Therapy in a Nutshell

10 Simple Lessons That Will Change Your Life

Patricia L. Bay, M.A.

Marriage, Family Therapist

Best wishes,

Dr. Patty Bay

ISBN   1-883952-07-7

Quotations Reprinted by Permission:

From the Introduction to "A Course in Miracles" © 1975 Foundation for Inner Peace.

Helen Keller Archives of the American Foundation for the Blind.

Excerpted with the permission of Simon & Schuster from "The Positive Principle Today" by Norman Vincent Peale. Copyright © 1976 by Dr. Norman Vincent Peale. (Also, reprinted by permission of Cake Eaters, Inc. from "Timeless Wisdom" a book of quotations compiled by Gary W. Fenchuk. Copyright © 1994, Revised 1995 by Cake Eaters, Inc.)

Reprinted with the permission of Simon & Schuster from "Thoughts from the Seat of the Soul" by Gary Zukav. Copyright © 1989, 1994 by Gary Zukav.

Reprinted by permission of HarperCollins Publishers, Inc. from "Seasons of Your Heart: Prayers and Reflections" by Macrina Wiederkehr. Revised and Expanded. Copyright © 1991 by Macrina Wiederkehr.

Reprinted by permission of G.P. Putnam's Sons from "Conversations With God - Book One" by Neale Donald Walsch. Copyright © 1995 by Neale Donald Walsch.

Scripture quotation from The Holy Bible (Revised Standard Version).

"Attitude" used by permission of Insight for Living, Anaheim, CA 92806 - from "Strengthening Your Grip" by Charles Swindoll, Word Publishing. Copyright ©1982 by Charles Swindoll.

An exhaustive effort has been made to clear all reprint permissions for this book. If any required acknowledgments have been omitted, it is unintentional. If notified, the publisher will be pleased to rectify any omission in future editions.

Publisher: Flashbacks Unlimited, L.L.C.
Cover and Book Design: Amy Long and Bonnie Huey
Author Photo Copyright © 2006 by T.A. Schmidt Photography

10 9 8 7 6 5 4

TO RICHARD,
my most intimate friend, lover,
partner, and husband,
for always believing in me;

and

to our children,
Tara and Ashley,
who teach me constantly about life;

and

to my parents,
Jack and Elaine Young,
with love, respect, and gratitude
for giving me a strong foundation.

ACKNOWLEDGMENTS

Every piece of work has people who provide support, help, and encouragement. This book has many. I would like to thank all those who believed in me and knew this book was a possibility and especially the following:

Richard Bay, Jack Young, and Sandra "Sam" Campbell Clark for reading every rough draft and final form of each chapter to give me their critiques, editing remarks, and tremendous encouragement.

Tony DeMarco, of Computer Learning Center, for being a major computer guru and rescuing this manuscript when my hard drive glitched, fouling the original and the backup copy that I was in the process of updating. With his computer genius he saved me from trying to recreate a year's worth of hard work.

Michael and Sue Arnold for their belief and support of this work in the publishing process. Their knowledge and expertise have been invaluable.

Susanne King for her expert editing of the final manuscript. Her straightforward and insightful comments were marvelous.

Most importantly, to my clients, past and present, who have allowed me the opportunity to grow with them on their personal journey. It is the wealth of knowledge and pain you have all shared with me that has helped me to create the lessons that I now share in this book.

NOTE:

The case histories and examples used in this book have been altered as to names and other identifying details to protect the privacy of the individuals involved.

Introduction

It was Sunday night about 10:00 o'clock. I was falling asleep cuddled into my husband, Richard. I was just drifting off when I startled awake. I had very clearly seen a book in front of me. I looked at it closely and saw the title, "Therapy In A Nutshell, 10 Simple Lessons That Will Change Your Life." What woke me was seeing my name printed at the bottom of the front cover. As I lay there, acutely awake now, I felt charged with energy even though it wasn't long before this that I was ready to go to sleep.

I closed my eyes and visualized the book in front of me again. This time I opened it to the Contents page and saw chapters that titled all the primary lessons that I teach to my clients in my private practice and in workshops. It all made such perfect sense. I was jazzed.

I unwrapped Richard's arm from across my body and slipped out of bed. He mumbled something like, "What's wrong...where are you going?" I explained the vision to him and he sleepily replied, "Oh." He wasn't really shocked because I had done things like this before. Once I choreographed a clogging dance in a dream, woke up, and wrote the whole thing down. It fit perfectly with the music and was one of our clogging exhibition team's favorite dances.

As I wrote out the vision I had seen, I thought, "Great title. God sure does have a sense of humor." I was back in bed a few minutes later.

I couldn't fall back to sleep. I returned to the den with my laptop computer and began writing with a sense of urgency. The drive to write this book began in the moment I saw the cover as I was falling asleep and stayed with me until it was finished. It poured out of me with power and purpose whenever I sat down to write. Sitting down to write was the hard part. Finding time to write between my private practice as a Marriage, Family Therapist, my busy family life with two, extremely active children, teaching clogging, and all the other interests in my life, was a real challenge.

This book was meant to be. The push to write it came from a Divine source, but the work evolved over 15 years of work in this field. I love teaching these lessons. They are part of me -- my belief system, my training, and my therapeutic skills.

When there was only one chapter left to write, I had a beautiful, spiritual experience. It was 3:30 in the morning, and I sat at my writing table in the dining room and stared out the window. The moonlight reflecting off the oak trees made the leaves shimmer in the breeze. I had just finished the last rewrite of Chapter 3 and had printed out the pages to add to the "hard copy" I was now holding in my hands.

I smiled as I remembered the comment my 9-year-old daughter, Ashley, had made that afternoon when she saw the book in printed form. "Mom, who will ever want to read a book this fat?" she stated indignantly. She looked at me steadily with her huge blue eyes and waited for my response. I got the impression that she was sure I had made a big mistake in the length of this book that she had heard so much about over the past year.

"It's not really a children's book, honey," I replied, hiding my smile behind a manufactured cough.

"Obviously!" Ashley announced and spun around to leave the room.

As I sat holding the printed pages and staring out the window, I listened to the quiet sounds of the house around me. I was trying to decide if I should go to bed or simply pull an "all-nighter" and launch into Chapter 10. My body was relaxing, and I could feel the sleepiness overtaking me. I decided to sit in the peace and quiet for just a few more moments.

"This is the gift. It is almost finished."

I felt the message more than I heard it. My entire being began to fill with an incredible sense of light, peacefulness, and love. The powerful, intense sensation radiated into me like a great beam of light from above. It was as though this beautiful beam of light was shining directly down onto my head and into my body -- encompassing my very soul. The tears streamed down my face, but I made no move to wipe them away.

I basked in the light for at least several minutes and found myself answering the loving Spirit that filled my soul. I thanked God for the inspiration and guidance for this gift -- this book that I was holding in my lap. I allowed myself to let go of any expectations or desires and simply put the possibilities into His hands.

After a time I felt the intense connection dissipate, but the sensation of Perfect Love remained. When I got into bed, I lay there for quite awhile and considered the obvious connection between this spiritual experience and the impetus to begin Chapter 10. This was the chapter that I wanted to be about the most important lesson of all -- The Road To Love.

The writing of this book has been a spiritual experience in its entirety, and I am eternally grateful for the opportunity. I give it to you with love.

Patty Bay

Contents

CHAPTER ONE

LOVE AND FEAR — THE ILLUSION OF SAFETY

"The opposite of love is fear,
but what is all-encompassing
can have no opposite."
--A Course In Miracles

At any given moment we can exist in a place of LOVE or a place of FEAR. It may appear that there are a multitude of places to exist emotionally, but they all relate to these -- Fear and Love -- if you understand the concept.

At first glance we say, "I know what it means to feel fear and love." But do we really? They seem like such simple terms for common human emotions. First we must understand Fear and how we choose to let it run our lives. Once we can see it, feel it, and understand it, then we can begin to learn about Love and how to create our lives from this wondrous place.

Learning about Fear first seems backwards. We do not want to be in a place of Fear. Why not start with Love, the thing we crave the most? It's easier to begin with what most people believe in and know. That is Fear. People tend to doubt that Love is real. Learning the differences between Love and Fear makes it easier to tell when you are in a place of Love or a place of Fear. It will then be easier to let go of Fear and exist in a place of Love.

"I can't let him in again," she sobbed, "if he does it again, I just don't know how I'd survive." I listened intently to the familiar ring of rejection, betrayal, and pain -- all expressions of fear. "When we got married I thought that we had committed to each other for life. We've had twenty-six good years together. We have a family, obligations -- a life together. How could he let go of everything that is important to us? I know he says it's over between them, and he wants to be with me and the kids, but how can I let him back in?" The look on her face spoke of a gut level of pain that tears at the soul.

I asked her a simple question, "Do you still love him?"

Her eyes flashed with anger as she spat out, "Do I look like a fool? I hate his guts right now!" She dissolved into tears again weakly stating the obvious, "Yes, I love him. It wouldn't hurt so badly if I didn't. I'm so scared, Patty, I'm so scared." She cried quietly into the tissue, and the energy seemed to drain out of her. I waited patiently.

Handing her the green velvet pillow from the sofa, I asked her to hold it in front of her chest like a shield. "Pretend that this is a bulletproof vest, and you're wearing it to protect yourself from getting shot." Madeline looked at me warily but cooperated with my demonstration. "If I leveled a gun at you right now and pulled the trigger, would your bulletproof vest be effective?"

"Of course not," she scoffed, "it's just a pillow."

"In your belief that it was a bulletproof vest, could you possibly have been fooled into believing you were safe from the gun?"

Madeline hesitated. "I guess I could have been fooled if I believed it really was a bulletproof vest." I had her interest now. The tears glistened in her eyes as she stared at me.

"Madeline," I said softly, "you wear your fear of Bill hurting you again like our false shield here. You have created an **Illusion of Safety** that allows you to believe that if you keep him at a distance, emotionally and physically, then it won't hurt as badly if he has another affair. If Bill betrayed you again, would it hurt?"

"I couldn't bear it. I'd die. I don't know what I'd do," Madeline replied in a whisper.

"Madeline, wouldn't it hurt even if you had your shield up and tried hard to keep him at a distance by not letting him back into your heart?"

"Yes."

"Then what do you have to lose? You know that you love him. You've decided to give him another chance. Your commitment to your family is strong -- the most important thing in your life. If you try to maintain your Illusion of Safety, what will happen?"

Madeline thought about it for a few moments, "I guess I'd be pushing him away, not letting him in. I guess that was part of the problem in the first place. How do I put down my shield? I'm so frightened. I'm confused, too. You say I need to feel these emotions, but how can I do that without being afraid?"

The light bulb was on. Now the real work could begin.

FEAR

Fear is alarm or agitation caused by the expectation or realization of danger. Realization of danger isn't the problem. When danger is put in our midst, we respond -- right or wrong, we respond. Even standing there catatonic is a response. Expectation is the key word. How do we learn to expect danger? What does it do to our lives when we expect something dangerous to happen?

Madeline realized the danger involved to her personal feelings of safety, security, and emotional stability when she found out her husband, Bill, was having an affair. When confronted with the situation, she responded the only way she knew how -- with Fear. There was a lot of screaming, crying, threats, and long, heartfelt discussions in both of their responses. If the realization of the danger were all Madeline had to deal with, it would have been over for her. Like someone yelling "BOO" from a hiding place and scaring her, she would have had an instant of alarm, an adrenaline rush, realized the danger was over, and been okay in a few minutes. The danger she felt from this crisis was not a joke and was not going to go away in a few minutes.

Madeline was now alerted to possible danger and immediately entered into an emotional space where she "expected" the danger to reoccur. This is instinctual. One of the ways we try to guarantee our personal safety is to be alert to possible harm. When walking down the street, it is good to be aware of your surroundings and stay alert. This type of hypervigilance becomes extremely subtle when it involves personal relationships.

In Madeline's expectation of further harm from Bill, she entered into a place of FEAR -- fear that the situation would reoccur and cause her further trauma. From her vulnerable and fragile place of trying to recover from the initial pain, she scrambled to build walls and put up shields to protect herself. Her fear seemed involuntary, beyond her control. This can feel extremely stressful when it occurs over a prolonged period of time.

When we are fearful, we do whatever we feel is necessary to protect ourselves. This tendency for "fight or flight" is instinctual. We easily understand this when the object of our fear is obvious, such as an attacker. When the thing we fear is more subtle, it is not as easy to accept. Madeline's fear of being hurt again by Bill left her struggling to feel safe. She began to rely on an *Illusion of Safety* in order to function in her day to day life.

An *Illusion of Safety* is the summation of all the defenses we create when we're trying to keep ourselves from being hurt again. A few of Madeline's defenses were as follows:

- Pushing Bill away with her anger, sarcasm, withdrawal, and pain.
- Being hypervigilant, staying constantly aware, of everything Bill did so as not to miss some possible misdeed that could mean he was back in the affair.
- Reading hidden meaning into everything he said.
- Testing him with repeat questions, worded differently, to see if he answered them consistently.
- Watching his eyes to notice where he turned his attentions when other women were around.
- Questioning her appearance, intelligence, and everything else about herself to correct any possible inadequacy before Bill could see it and then leave her.

- Constantly wanting reassurance from him but not believing him when he tried to give it to her because she didn't trust him anyway.

These defenses were supposed to make Madeline feel better so she could relax and go on with her life. Instead, she was like a knight going into battle with full armor. The spears and swords would not penetrate to hurt her, but neither would the soft touch of love be felt. This began a vicious cycle of fear. The more Madeline put energy into her *Illusion of Safety*, the more she focused on the trauma, hurt, and pain. Her misguided attempt to avoid the hurt again kept her from healing. Focusing on her fear pushed her ability to see and believe in Love even further away.

Madeline's *Illusion of Safety* was creating for her what she feared the most -- abandonment. She was pushing Bill away, isolating herself behind her armor and her walls, and becoming increasingly unavailable to her relationship with her husband. At some point Bill was bound to say, "I can't be in a relationship like this any longer." In a misguided attempt to meet his needs he would leave or have another affair.

At that point, Madeline could say, "See, I knew this would happen." She would feel justified in her defenses and blame Bill for abandoning her again.

Some people put up walls and shields intending to take them down when the danger is past and the trauma has healed. Others create these defenses with no intention of ever letting the walls down and feel completely justified in their actions. They decide this was a lesson life intended them to learn. The walls and shields stay in place and become thicker and heavier with each of life's difficult experiences. This is existing in a place of *FEAR*. To put it simply, a life lived from a constant place of fear is horrible. There is an alternative.

THE WALLS WE HIDE BEHIND
"The Illusion of Safety"

EXPERIENCES AFFECT FEAR

Not all walls are from current life traumas. Some of our walls originate in childhood. When a child lives with love and safety, that child learns to trust. When children live with fear, they learn to put up walls. The more prolonged and difficult the traumas, the thicker and taller the walls. We carry our walls into adulthood and then expect or fear that those situations may occur again. We are simply trying to protect ourselves from harm. We experience problems when these walls stand between us and someone with whom we want to be close. The other person feels our fear and the sensation of being shut out.

Remember the crayon boxes we had when we were kids? The box of 64 with the sharpener in the back. All of the sharp crayons sitting smartly in precise order smell wonderful when the box is opened. Now they make boxes of 120 crayons of many varying shades. Let's use one of these new boxes to illustrate how we use Fear.

Let's assume that our crayon box represents our experiences in life. We'll assume that we are all born into this world with some crayons in our box. We can put this assumption into any spiritual framework you like. Maybe God gives us certain crayons to deal with when we are born into this world. Maybe we carry crayons from past life experiences. We can pick up a few during a stressful, difficult pregnancy and birth. Our first experience in our entry into the world may be some guy in a mask slapping us on the bottom while he hangs us upside down. That alone can put a couple of angry crayons in our box, and we do not even have verbal skills yet to talk about it.

As we grow and experience our world, we add crayons to our box. If we feel welcomed and loved, we may add a few beautiful, soft colors. If we grow up in a safe, secure environment, we add more beautiful crayons. If someone harms us in some way, we may add painful, ugly colors to our box. Some experiences add a crayon for awhile only to have a different experience remove that crayon and replace it with a different color.

A dog bites a child and she puts a couple of crayons into her box. Now whenever she sees a dog, she colors this current experience with her old "dogs are bad" crayons. She is afraid of dogs. Later, she gets a puppy of her own and realizes that not all dogs are bad. She puts a few "dogs are nice" crayons into her box. If she's lucky, she can throw out the old "dogs are bad" crayons and only remember that they used to be there. She is left with the reality that some dogs are nice and some dogs are not. If she can't throw the old, negative crayons out, maybe she'll be able to put the "dogs are nice" crayons in front of the "dogs are bad" crayons so that her first reaction to a dog will be a positive one.

If the little girl grows up to be a very aware, introspective adult, she may learn that she has a few "dogs are bad" crayons, but they are overshadowed by her "dogs are nice" crayons. If she does happen to grab one of the old negative crayons, as she might when faced with the same situation or breed of dog that bit her, she consciously tries not to grab the old trauma colors and purposely colors this current experience with her more positive crayons. Hopefully, her old trauma crayons will have motivated her to learn how to deal with dogs from a place of Love while staying aware of possible dangers.

The possibilities for combinations of colors, adding and replacing colors, are endless. Each person's box of experiences is unique. Often, when a person enters into therapy, they are trying to say, "My crayon box is all messed up." They may try to say that the world is full of nasty, ugly colors, or they may ask why they tend to color their experiences with ugly colors. Sometimes I hear them understand that their own personal crayon box is filled with trauma crayons. They want to get rid of the trauma crayons so they can color their world and see their world as beautiful. Sometimes they can see that not everyone has difficult, ugly colors, and they begin to doubt themselves. "What is wrong with me? Why can't I trust people? Why can't I express my emotions? Why do my relationships fail? Why do I hurt so much?"

In good therapy you learn to identify the crayons in your box. How did they get there? How do you use your personal crayons to color your current life experiences? Can you identify the negative and positive crayons in your box? Do you reach for the nasty ones even when you have beautiful crayons there for your use? Do you color a present day experience with an inappropriate, old crayon? How do you allow yourself to use your positive crayons and still utilize the lessons you learned from your difficult experiences?

If a child is sexually molested, there is a tendency to put many ugly crayons in the box. When the child enters into an adult relationship, he or she may color a partner with some of these ugly crayons, even though the partner didn't have a thing to do with putting those traumas in the crayon box. Some of the crayons could be labeled "people can't be trusted," "sex is dirty," "I'm dirty," "you say you love me, but that just means you want to use me."

Therapy can help identify the who, what, where, why, when, and how of the crayons that are causing problems in your current life. With some hard work, you may discard a few, replace a few, and learn to place the ones that you cannot discard, in the back of the box where they aren't readily available. A very aware person will learn to recognize when they are pulling out an old, ugly crayon and begin to consciously put it back and choose a bright, newer crayon from the front of the box.

We can call the negative, ugly crayons that we put in our box, "fear crayons." We put them there and keep them there to help us feel safe. They are the evidence that we "expect" something dangerous to happen, and we want to be ready when it does. We don't want to be unprepared. We would feel foolish if "it" -- whatever "it" is -- happened to us again, and we didn't color it correctly. We want to be ready to protect ourselves. We use these crayons to color our shields and walls that are our *Illusions of Safety*.

When Madeline went through her trauma with Bill, she put a whole line of new crayons in her box. They could have been labeled "don't trust him" and "everyone is out to hurt me" and "commitment is not real." Until she began to heal her pain and fear, Madeline first pulled out these crayons to color every experience. She seemed angry, bitter, cynical, and depressed. She was in a place of Fear.

This seems confusing. How do we learn from our past experiences without constantly existing in a place of Fear? Some people do it naturally. I have seen molest survivors in therapy who do not have impaired trusting abilities or sexual problems. They have been able to teach their own children how to protect themselves from "bad people" in the world, without jading their children into viewing that everyone is bad and someone to fear.

The difference that I have observed between the

people who survive their traumas and those who continue to be victimized is that the survivors seem to grasp the concept that the world is basically a place of Love. They realize that "bad" things can happen to good, loving people when someone else, like an offender, relates to the world from a place of Fear. Of course, a vast majority of people do not, yet, come into therapy using the language of Fear and Love, but they express the same concept in their own words and spiritual beliefs.

It doesn't mean that the survivors of trauma were never angry, hurt, depressed, resentful, and fearful. They went through the usual path of healing that most everyone experiences, and that includes these difficult emotions. Somehow they returned to a place of Love and began relating to others from that place once more.

LOVE

The alternative to Fear is Love. Sometimes love is a harder thing to see clearly. Funny isn't it, how fear is rather easy to define, feel, and notice, but love is far more subtle? It is beyond our earthly abilities to even begin to fathom the vast complexities and possibilities that exist in a state of Love. Love is far more than a feeling we have about someone else. It is a spiritual place of being that encompasses all that is.

If Fear is not of Love, then Fear cannot be part of all that is. Therefore, Fear does not truly exist and is only an illusion we create for ourselves to try to put some understanding to our world. Why is it then that Fear feels so real when we are stuck in the middle of it? Why do we tend to doubt Love, often believing that the place of Fear is what is real and the place of Love is the illusion? We're good at it, aren't we? How do we ever get so mixed up? How do we begin to turn it back around, as it is meant to be, and see Love as our only true reality and Fear as the thing we invent to explain the things we don't understand?

Let's begin with what we, as human beings, have long defined as Love -- Love for another. This can be defined as "an intense affection for another person based on personal or familial ties"; "a strong affection for or attachment to another person based on regard or shared experiences or interests"; or "an intense attraction to another person based mainly on sexual desire."

See if you can think of a relationship that isn't mixed with fear. Notice how you feel about your mate, your child, a coworker, a close friend. Do you feel fear mixed with those feelings? Do you feel the quiet, peaceful, contented emotions we have come to call love?

When we are in a state of Love, we usually feel calm. Feelings of being personally threatened diminish. We relax. We let our shields down. We see the world from a more centered place. The real lesson in life is learning how to exist in this state of Love a majority of the time. The secret is recognizing when you aren't there -- when you are in a state of Fear.

To begin your awareness of when you are in a state of Love and when you are in a state of Fear, ask yourself where you are this very moment. You may recognize it and you may not. During any situation, especially difficult ones, ask yourself, "Am I in a state of Love or Fear, right now?"

Sheryl, a 38-year-old teacher and school counselor, came to me for therapy to treat stress and burnout regarding her job. After some exploration, we discovered that she actually enjoyed her work with children and families, and this was not causing a majority of the stress. Sheryl felt inadequate around her coworkers and especially with her supervisor, a rather cold, unemotional woman with an air of superiority. Sheryl found herself distraught, to the point of feeling ill, whenever her supervisor would call her in for a meeting.

When Sheryl began to see her nervousness and apprehension as FEAR, changes began to occur. She was able to identify her fears in the following exercise:

IDENTIFYING FEAR

1. I AM WORRIED ABOUT THE FOLLOWING SITUATION:

_____

_____

2. I FEAR THE FOLLOWING POSSIBILITIES: _____

_____

_____

3. HOW DOES MY FEAR MAKE ME BEHAVE SO THAT I CREATE MY "ILLUSION OF SAFETY?"

_____

_____

4. HOW CAN I DEAL WITH THESE SAME CONCERNS WITH LOVE?

_____

_____

Sheryl answered the exercise questions as follows:

1.   I am worried about meeting with my supervisor.

2.   I am afraid that:
   - I will look inadequate.
   - I will say something stupid.
   - She will intimidate me, and I will do something stupid like cry or get angry or babble unintelligent junk.
   - Afterwards I will feel depressed and I hate that.
   - I will quit my job (I can't afford to quit) out of pure anger and frustration (and maybe to "show her" that she can't control me).
   - If I quit my job, what will my husband think of me. (I can't leave him with all the financial burdens.)
   - If I quit my job, my mother will, once again, tell me how I should have done it differently.
   - I wouldn't like myself very much if I quit. I'd feel like a frightened rabbit who bolted from the fox.
   - If I don't quit, my supervisor will fire me because it will be so obvious that I'm totally inadequate.
   - No one would want to hire me again.
   - I'll lose all sense of my identity, get horribly depressed, and crawl under some rock and disappear.

3.   I try to keep myself safe by getting really nervous and anxious before I have to deal with my supervisor. I guess I think this will make me be prepared somehow. I also push her away outside our working

environment. I avoid her and keep from getting to know her because I feel unsafe around her.

4.   How can I handle this situation with LOVE instead of FEAR?
"I DON'T HAVE A CLUE.....HEELLLPPPP!!!!!"

Sheryl brought the finished exercise into her next session. She was clearly able to identify her fears of inadequacy and abandonment. She also isolated some "mother issues" that we would work on if necessary.

I asked Sheryl to read her answers aloud. "Who is it that creates these fears?" I challenged her.

"I create them?" she replied in that hesitant manner that indicated to me she knew the correct answer but did not yet believe it.

"For what purpose? What does your fear do for you?"

"Well, I guess if I allow myself to be afraid, then I put up an emotional shield before I go into the supervisor's office. If she's nasty, I feel like I'm ready for it and I won't be so vulnerable." Sheryl was sitting straighter in her chair with a bright, alert look on her face.

I smiled slowly and simply said, "Does it work?"

Almost bouncing out of her chair, Sheryl cried, "NO! NO!" I get frightened and end up feeling like I'm seven years old. I'm not prepared for anything in that state. I can't believe how I've been sabotaging myself all this time."

"This actually has nothing to do with your super-

visor. *She exists in her own emotional state that may or may not have anything to do with yours. Isn't it interesting how you have been giving her the power over this situation this whole time. If you are ready, you can take your power back. You do this by letting go of your fear and moving into a place of love."*

Sheryl looked at me for a moment. "I just don't get that part. I can see the fear. I can understand where it comes from and what I'm trying to do with it, but how do I let it go?"

"You have accomplished the first step really well. You have IDENTIFIED your fear. Now it is time for the second step, UNDERSTAND and RESPECT your fear. We create fear for a reason, and we need to take a close look at this window into ourselves. There is no need to run from fear. Stop and take a look at it and acknowledge to yourself what it is that you fear. Don't over analyze it, put it down as stupid, or stress about it. Simply look at it. Can you do that now?"

Sheryl slowly began verbalizing what she knew. "I guess I do understand that I'm afraid that I am inadequate and as soon as someone sees this hidden part of me, they will leave me."

"Great!" I said with enthusiasm. "What would happen if you just let that be? If you told yourself, 'Okay, I guess I'm afraid of those things.' Would the world come to an end simply because you acknowledged your fears?"

"No," she replied with a reflective look in her eyes.

"Now for the final step. You have identified, understood, and respected your fears. If you were not

afraid, how do you think you would behave with your supervisor?"

"I'd believe in myself. I would go into her office and simply see what she wants from me. I'd listen, without my heart pounding, and use my experience, knowledge, and education to answer her. I would be able to interact with her on an equal level."

"If at any time during this conversation, you began to feel afraid, what would you do?"

"I'd try to acknowledge my fear to myself and continue to love myself. That's it. THAT'S IT, isn't it? This isn't about loving her as much as it's about loving me. I don't think I've ever loved me."

Sheryl and I spent some time working on her abilities, self-esteem, and learning to love herself. She is now much more relaxed at work and has actually gained a productive working relationship with her supervisor. Of course, her issues of feeling inadequate and fearing abandonment creep into her consciousness at times, but she is able to identify these fears and not let them control how she feels about herself.

This Fear and Love thing is so simple yet so complex. It reminds me of how I feel when someone says "just do this" or "let it go" or "stop feeling that way." It would be nice to "just stop and begin to do it differently," if you could even see what "it" is. However, it isn't always that easy. How do you stop doing something that is unreal and just an illusion, called Fear, and begin to do something that is real, but difficult to define, called Love? Seems like heavy, esoteric stuff, doesn't it? Actually it is not. When the "light bulb" goes on for you, and you can see the Love that I'm talking about, you'll laugh at the simplicity of it all.

CHAPTER TWO

INTIMACY —
LEARNING TO TRUST

*"The best and most beautiful
things in the world cannot
be seen nor even touched
but just felt in the heart."*
-- Helen Keller

Developing healthy relationships is one of life's greatest challenges. The quality of your relationships can determine the level of fulfillment and happiness you experience in life. Some of our biggest fears surface in response to relationship issues. Most people fear rejection and abandonment more than anything else, besides maybe death. For many, being left by someone you love tremendously is more scary than the thought of dying.

What is jealousy? The fear of being left or of not being good enough in comparison with someone else. What is the feeling of being taken for granted? The fear of not being important to someone or the fear of rejection.

I often find that many people do not have a clue how to develop relationships. Many are either in an unhealthy relationship or between love interests. Some find themselves moving along unconsciously recreating previous mistakes. Others consciously try not to make the same blunders and instead make new mistakes by doing the exact opposite.

Sandra came to me for marital therapy with her second husband, Robert. She cared for him but felt extremely bored and trapped in a passionless marriage. She described Robert as a good man, hardworking, reliable, and extremely predictable. He loved her very much, and she felt guilty that she did not return his deep love. In individual therapy Sandra and I explored her past relationships and her reasons for marrying Robert.

Sandra explained that her first husband was an intensely passionate, spontaneous, exciting man. Unfortunately he was also an alcoholic who was usually unemployed. After nine years of trying to change husband number one, Sandra left the marriage. His passion could not make up for the intense feelings of insecurity and fear brought on by his alcoholism and instability. Sandra vowed that she would find a man who was a good provider and didn't drink. She wanted someone with whom she could feel safe. She found that man in Robert. Now, almost four years into this relationship, she was bored to tears.

"I thought I was being so smart by not recreating the previous mistakes of my first marriage," Sandra sighed. "It didn't occur to me that I could be miserable in a different way by creating a relationship exactly opposite of what I had before. I guess this goes with that saying 'be careful what you ask for because you just might get it.'"

Sandra had done what a lot of people tend to do when they leave a bad relationship. She did a "one-eighty." Meaning, she did a 180 degree turn from where she was in order to end up in a new place.

Robert was a polar opposite of her first husband and that was all that Sandra could see at the time. It seemed perfect to her because Robert was not an alcoholic and he was financially stable. Now, with some distance from her first marriage, Sandra could see that Robert had some characteristics that were challenging to their relationship.

Sandra and Robert did a lot of work together to create some excitement and passion in their marriage. Robert worked individually on his perfectionistic control issues that caused him to be uptight and stuffy. Sandra decided to stay in this marriage because she did feel safe and secure. They were able to make some adjustments that helped her feel more satisfied with Robert.

If Sandra had entered into therapy between these two relationships, we would have worked on how to develop a healthy relationship. Learning to take things slowly by taking people through the trusting levels is easy. It doesn't matter if the person you are learning about is a potential love interest, coworker, or friend.

As you learn the following trusting levels, think of the existing relationships you have that fit into each level. Think about past relationships. What level were they when they started? Where are these relationships now? If a relationship ended, what was the trusting level at the end? You may have thought some were deeper than they turned out to be.

TRUSTING LEVELS

LEVEL ONE .... ACQUAINTANCES

LEVEL TWO .... FRIENDS

LEVEL THREE .... GOOD FRIENDS

LEVEL FOUR .... BEST FRIENDS

THE WALL

LEVEL FIVE .... INTIMACY

Level One
ACQUAINTANCES

These are the people you know, but not really well. You may know their name or where they work, such as the mail carrier or the grocery clerk, but you usually don't know much else about them. This is the beginning stage of a potentially deeper friendship, or maybe as far as this relationship will go. Most people have a lot of acquaintances.

Level Two
FRIENDS

You know more about friends than the acquaintances in your life. You probably know their first and last name, whether they are married, or if they have children. You probably run into friends at social gatherings, or you may work with them on a daily basis. You enjoy chatting with them but usually keep things on a pleasant, surface level of conversation. These are the people who ask, "How are you?" and you almost always answer, "Fine, fine. How are you?"

Level Three
GOOD FRIENDS

How much time you spend with a person begins to distinguish the "Level Two, Friends" from the good friends described in this level. These are the people you go to lunch with, invite to gatherings, and see fairly regularly. You usually move in the same circles, such as school, work, or your neighborhood. You know a lot about these people, and they know many things about you. Your conversations are on a deeper level of communication than with friends, but generally things are kept pretty light.

If a good friend moves out of your circle of influence, you often times lose touch with one another. There are usually a lot of people on your holiday card list that fit this description.

Level Four
BEST FRIENDS

These are the people who know most things about you and you know most things about them. You go out of your way to spend time with these people and miss them when you haven't seen them. These are the friends you think of calling in good times and bad, and you rely on them in your life. The loss or absence of these people leaves a void in your heart.

If a "best friend" moves away or goes to work or school somewhere else, more effort is usually made to stay in touch with one another. If this effort slips away, there are often times feelings of loss or hurt involved.

THE WALL

The wall between levels four and five, which will be discussed in a moment, is a healthy thing. Some people have no wall whatsoever, and people too easily progress into the intimate area of level five. Everyone knows someone, perhaps yourself, who tells anyone and everyone their intimate, personal feelings and situations. These are the people who do not have a healthy wall in place.

Have you ever overheard the person in line before you telling the grocery store clerk some health or sex life detail, and you feel like cringing? How do you feel when someone you think of as an acquaintance or friend begins telling you intimate life details? It can be embarrassing. Knowing how far to let someone in takes thought and consideration. It should take time and consistency before a person is allowed into the deeper, intimate levels of your life.

Other people have a misplaced wall. It doesn't exist between levels four and five, but somewhere higher. I often see people in therapy with a wall between levels two and three. They have acquaintances and friends, but no one that really knows them because their wall keeps everyone out. Often times they enter into therapy with their spouses saying that they don't feel close or connected. Sometimes they come to therapy by themselves realizing that they have never developed any deep, lasting relationships. This is a trusting impairment, and therapy can be very useful in resolving the underlying issues.

Level Five
INTIMACY

These are the people whom you truly love and trust. If you have two or three people in this coveted area, consider yourself fortunate. You feel heart connected and have complete trust and honesty with these people. They know the skeletons in your closet, your deep dark secrets, your strengths and weaknesses, and you know theirs. Despite complete knowledge of the other, there is unconditional love and acceptance. This type of intimacy has nothing to do with sexual intimacy, but the sexual relationships that exist in this arena are the healthiest ones. It is here that the closest and most rewarding relationships exist. It is at this level that most people want their marriages to be.

Level five relationships are not perfect, just committed. There can be heartache, strife, and hurt in a level five relationship because we are all human and we make mistakes as we go through the challenges of life. A level five relationship differs from those of a lesser commitment in that there exists a willingness to work through the problems.

Level five people can be your closest friend, your spouse, or a relative. There are even parent/child level five relationships. These would vary slightly, though, in that parents should not share some of the intimate details of their adult life with their children. Often times teenagers will feel like their parent or parents are their closest friend, but still may not share absolutely everything.

Sometimes therapy is the first level five relationship a person experiences. This is not quite like relationships in the world, though, because the therapist/client relationship is a one-way interaction. The therapist ends up knowing most things about the client, but the client usually knows very little about the therapist. This can be a safe place to experience the feeling of being completely open and honest with someone. If you have a therapist who is accepting, nonjudgmental, and appropriately caring, this will be a positive experience in trusting.

CHARACTERISTICS OF A HEALTHY LEVEL FIVE RELATIONSHIP

Honesty
Reliability
Ability to keep confidences
Ability to listen
Nonjudgmental
Accepting
Open-minded
Ability to share feelings
Commitment to the relationship
Willingness to work through problems
Some likes/dislikes in common
Mutual caring
Sensitivity
Personal responsibility

No one is ever perfect with the above characteristics. A person with good level five qualities will try to be consistent. More importantly, when a problem arises, the commitment is there to work things through. Level five relationships are far from perfect, they are just tenacious. The "stick-to-itiveness" and willingness to grow are what really count.

It is important to know that not every person is capable of being a true level five. The ability to accept personal responsibility for mistakes is imperative. Giving, receiving, trusting, and acceptance also typify a healthy person in a level five relationship.

Sometimes we find ourselves in a one-way level five or with any of the levels for that matter. This can happen when one person has more of the healthy characteristics than the other person. It can also occur when a person has more energy invested in you than you have in that person, or vice versa.

With many couples in marital therapy one person is open, loving, and accepting. The other is closed off, doesn't express feelings, and appears judgmental and critical. The first person gives and wants a level five relationship, and for whatever reason, the mate cannot or will not reciprocate. Sometimes it happens with friends. Some people want more than you can or want to give. Maybe you think of them as "good friends," but they keep acting like level five, "intimate friends." You may not like their beliefs or attitudes and have chosen to keep them at a safer distance. Conflict may arise when they demand too much or question why you don't feel about them as they do about you.

Shirley was concerned about her relationship with her closest friend, Lindsey. Both were adult women with husbands and children. Each led a busy life working their careers and managing their households. Shirley said that Lindsey was constantly irritated with her for not putting more time into their friendship. Lindsey called Shirley daily and wanted to have long, involved phone calls, and Shirley just didn't feel she had the time to talk for an hour each evening.

Their friendship was more and more strained as Lindsey demanded more than Shirley could or wanted to give to the relationship. Even when they did have some time together, Lindsey's feelings of rejection and abandonment set the tone for the interaction. Shirley found herself alternating between feelings of guilt for not fulfilling Lindsey's expectations and feelings of irritation at her possessive, demanding stance.

Shirley came into therapy stating that everything was confusing and complicated with this friendship, and she wanted help figuring out what she was doing wrong. In fact, Lindsey had told Shirley that she had a problem being close to people and that she should get some help.

When Shirley learned the Trusting Levels, she was able to see that she did not actively take her friendship with Lindsey through these levels. When Shirley first met Lindsey at a school function for their children, Lindsey introduced herself, and the two women talked during the event. Lindsey started calling Shirley and invited her to do things and get together.

Lindsey set the tone for the depth of sharing and interacting. Shirley found herself "going along for the ride." Lindsey didn't seem to notice that she shared deep, intimate secrets and feelings, and Shirley tended to listen without sharing much about herself.

In looking back at the progression of this friendship, Shirley could now see that she had been uncomfortable from the beginning. Lindsey had placed the relationship far too quickly at a level five. If Shirley had known then what she was learning now, she would have slowly gotten to know Lindsey. She would have noticed that Lindsey did not have very good boundaries, and Shirley would have held the friendship at a less intense level such as FRIEND or GOOD FRIEND.

The secret is to allow people in your life to exist in the place in which they are capable of being. You may carry around unnecessary anger and resentment at a friend that you wish would behave as a level five with you. You trust with your deep, inner self and continually feel betrayed by the friend's inability to keep your confidences. You get angry and keep feeling attacked by the untrustworthiness. What would happen if you backed this person up to a level four or three? The secret is to love and have fun and to involve people in your life to the extent they are capable of honoring.

I often see adults who feel very wounded by their own parents. They have a belief, or should I say a desire, to have their family be level five people in their lives. They continually feel disappointed when their parents judge, criticize, and belittle who they are. They have a deep longing for the trust and unconditional love that they know exists in close, healthy relationships and feel cheated and abused when it does not exist in theirs. When these adults stop demanding, wishing, and expecting their parents to be the level five relationships they long for, a burden they have carried all their lives can be alleviated. With this attitude shift they can begin to view their parents in a more appropriate level, one that fits their parents' communication skills and awareness abilities. They stop expecting more. This allows them to love their parents for who they are and what they are capable of being, without the continual disappointment and feelings of inadequacy. This does not mean that they should withdraw, clam up, and stop sharing their lives. It only means that the level of sharing changes from one of an intimate sharing of hopes and fears to a safer level of communication.

Sometimes people learn the trusting levels and a deep sadness sets in. They realize that they have married someone who is not yet capable of level five behavior, and that is where they want their life's mate to exist with them. At this point there are choices to be made. Is the person willing to enter into therapy and learn how to trust and open up? Is this person someone you truly love and admire and want to have a level five relationship with? Are you willing to create a healthy relationship that exists on a different level and seek out appropriate level five relationships elsewhere?

The concept of trusting levels is very useful to people in the dating world. It is equally effective for teenagers or someone leaving a long term relationship. Moving someone through the trusting levels allows time to really know a person. If you've made a commitment to yourself to not allow a sexual relationship to begin until you feel a strong level five relationship has developed, you will save a lot of heartache and avoid the perils that exist in the world of casual sex. Think about what types of things you would do with a "friend" or a "good friend." Go out for coffee, go to a movie, take a walk, or talk on the phone. Sitting alone in someone's living room with them is something you probably would reserve for a level four or five person. When you first meet someone, do the things appropriate for the beginning levels of a friendship. It doesn't matter if this relationship is going to be "just a friend" or a prospective sexual partner or life's mate. Treat everyone the same in the beginning, and you will form deeply developed interpersonal relationships.

Trusting is one of the important elements in any relationship. The depth to which a person can trust affects the quality of love between two people. The skills to trust wisely and appropriately as shown in the "Trusting Levels" allow one to relax and let go of fear. Relationships experienced from a place of Love feel wonderful. Once experienced, it is a feeling you will cherish and always want to have in your life. It will be felt in the heart.

CHAPTER THREE

HEALTHY PATTERNS

"There is a basic law that like attracts like.
Negative thinking definitely attracts
negative results. Conversely, if a person
habitually thinks optimistically
and hopefully, his positive thinking
sets in motion creative forces —
and success instead of eluding him
flows toward him."
--Norman Vincent Peale (adapted)

Everyone feels stuck in a rut at some time during life. Things get routine and boring which creates a desire to "do something differently." Change is an interesting thing -- often a good thing. Some people fight change and find comfort in the monotony. My father has always liked to keep things the same. Every day of his life, at least for as long as I can remember (and I can picture this back to age three), he has eaten Rice Krispies cereal and a banana for breakfast. You would think after 40 years of "snap, crackle, and pop" he would "snap, crackle, and pop," but he simply says, "I like it."

The routines and habits we become accustomed to can be called "patterns" of behavior. These patterns tend to become more and more entrenched into our repertoire of responses to people and situations until, often times, we are not consciously aware that we are doing them. It is healthy to occasionally bring these behaviors back to a conscious awareness level so that we can look at them. This gives us the opportunity to grow.

If you look at human behavior as similar to an iceberg, you visualize how your awareness level can be so important. Picture an iceberg floating in the ocean. You've heard of the saying "that's just the tip of the iceberg." That saying refers to the fact that as the iceberg floats in the water, most of the mass is underneath the water's surface and only a small portion, the tip of the iceberg, shows above the waterline.

The portion of the iceberg above the waterline equates with your "conscious thoughts and behaviors" -- the thoughts and behaviors of which you are aware. The much larger portion of the iceberg is still underwater. This hidden part compares to your unconscious thoughts and behaviors. Even though you cannot see this part, meaning you are not consciously aware of these thoughts and behaviors, it can be extremely powerful. The unseen part of an iceberg can sink a huge ocean liner just as your unconscious responses can create havoc and disaster in your life.

The goal in learning to recognize your patterns of behavior is to "lower your water line" so that more of who you really are, deep down inside, becomes available to your conscious control. In the ocean, the more visible the iceberg is, the more accurately a ship can steer clear of disaster. However, a good captain knows there is usually much more beneath the surface than appearances may display.

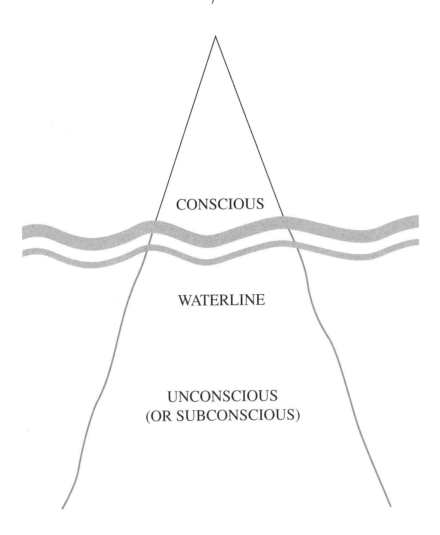

CONSCIOUS

WATERLINE

UNCONSCIOUS
(OR SUBCONSCIOUS)

An easy place to begin to recognize some of your own unconscious, or subconscious, patterns is to look at how you tend to respond when you are threatened. There are many types of threats to a person's feelings of safety. Some threats make you fearful for your physical safety and some make you fearful for your emotional safety. The intensity of your response is usually, though not always, proportional to your perception of the intensity of the threat and its probability of causing you harm.

The unconscious, automatic, reflexive response we give to a threat is called a "defense mechanism." There are many different types of defense mechanisms, and it is very beneficial to learn to recognize which type you generally choose when you feel threatened. Once a defense mechanism reaches your conscious level of behavior -- rises above your waterline -- you have the opportunity to achieve voluntary control over your reactions. (At the end of this chapter is a list of defense mechanisms to help you identify your typical responses.)

SELF-GROWTH

A man came to see me for therapy and stated, "My girlfriend told me that she left me because I was not into self-growth. At first that made me pretty angry. Then I stopped to think about what she said and realized I didn't have a clue what she was talking about. What in the hell does everyone mean when they talk about this self-growth junk?"

"Self-growth" refers to the process of accessing your strengths and weaknesses in an honest, forthright manner and then learning what you need to do to believe in your strengths and improve your weaknesses. This process of becoming more conscious of who you really are deep inside -- not just what your thoughts and behaviors are on the surface -- can be called "self-growth."

The "self" part of "self-growth" refers to the acceptance of personal responsibility in this development process. In other words, no one is making you do it. If being forced to grow counted, it would be called something like "wife-induced growth," or whoever was making you do the growing.

The "growth" in "self-growth" refers to an increasing awareness and development of new, healthier behaviors and patterns in your life. The idea is to check out who you are now by getting past all the defense mechanisms that you've learned to use (so you don't have to look at who you really are). You then add all the new and improved versions of feelings, thoughts, and behaviors to your repertoire of responses. Piece of cake! If we break the whole process down into understandable, manageable steps, it really is easier than it sounds.

People begin the process of "lowering their water-line," or becoming conscious of how they deal with themselves and others, from many different levels of development. Most people can fit into a reference that I call "Emotional Growth Levels." These levels start with people who are just beginning to discover who they are and how they function emotionally. They progress to highly, emotionally developed people who recognize that self-growth is a lifetime process.

People do not fit neatly into one of these "Emotional Growth Levels" because we are individuals and any type of diagnostic category defies inclusion of the masses. You may find that you vary from one level to the next depending on the situation or the relationship involved. Use these levels as a tool to stimulate your thinking and awareness of who you are. Figuring out how you do not fit into the levels can be just as valuable as discovering how you do fit.

Within each therapy level there are also many sub-levels of progression. There are not any concrete measuring tools that can tell you when you've entered into the next level. It can be a subtle and very personal experience. Awareness is the key to understanding where you are now and where you would like to progress to from that point.

It is very common for people to be better at recognizing where someone else falls into the "Emotional Growth Levels" than they are at noticing into which level they fall. This is similar to how many people give great advice and can help others make very positive changes, yet show little ability to manage their own lives or "practice what they preach."

The "Emotional Growth Levels" refer to how you handle your own feelings and emotions, as well as your ability to express them and create positive, healthy changes. There is no shame, stigma, self-importance, or honor in where you begin to grow. We are each on our own journey in this thing we call life, but we all need a little help sometimes in expanding and changing directions.

EMOTIONAL GROWTH LEVELS

LEVEL ONE

- Little ability to identify feelings, except possibly anger; sometimes can express positive emotions such as happiness, excitement, and love.
- Difficulty talking about personal issues.
- Difficulty accepting responsibility; usually uses the defense mechanisms of denial and blaming but can

be adept at all the defense mechanisms.

- Usually feels somewhat forced into changing, either by a loved one, the courts, or by the behavior of someone else.
- Demonstrates little ability to change difficult problems.

Lisa came to therapy with complaints of severe marital problems. After working on her fears and issues for several weeks, we decided to ask her husband, Tom, to join us. It took four or five weeks for him to agree to attend a session with Lisa. He kept telling her that it was her problem, and he was not going to get off work, or flex a lunch hour, to accommodate her. He also had a long list of things that if she "just did" then everything would be fine. When these blaming defense mechanisms fell short, he would launch into others such as "therapists don't know what they're doing" or "I'm not talking to a stranger (and a woman at that) about our dirty laundry" or "I don't believe in therapy" or "if I can't handle my own family, then I'm not much of a man." Tom finally showed up when she told him that she and the children were leaving if he did not come to her next session.

Tom sat with his arms crossed on the couch and clarified in no uncertain terms that he did not want to be here, did not believe in this stupid touchy-feely stuff, and only came because Lisa forced him. As his wife sat near him in the chair, she looked anxious and embarrassed. I watched the fear in Tom's eyes.

Tom had definite "Level One" characteristics. I did not enter into his defense mechanisms by debating the merits of therapy with him. I tried to create a safe and non-confrontational atmosphere by acknowledging his statements and asking him to explain the strengths and weaknesses that he perceived in the relationship. We kept the discussion fairly devoid of emotions and conversed in the intellectual framework in which he was comfortable.

Therapy needs to start wherever the client is comfortable. If I had immediately asked Tom to identify feelings or tried to teach him how, he would have been very uncomfortable. He needed time to adjust and develop some trust of me and the situation before his armor could be confronted. This process can move along quickly or take many, many sessions. Developing the ability to simply begin to look at emotions is productive therapy in and of itself.

LEVEL TWO

- Some ability to identify feelings.
- Little or no ability to talk about these feelings.
- Little ability to create positive emotional changes.
- Personally seeks out therapy or agrees to come because of the hurt and pain. Sometimes can identify what is hurting, but does not usually know where to go from there.

Leigh, age 17, was brought to therapy by her mother. She came fairly willingly after her mother noticed that Leigh seemed depressed. She admitted to her mother, and to me, that she was stressed with school and very down since a girl she knew at school committed suicide.

When Leigh's mother left the room, we began to explore her feelings about school and the loss of her friend. She had some trouble putting her difficult emotions into words. I asked her to explain how she knew she was stressed and feeling down. Leigh was able to describe behaviors such as an inability to concentrate, crying easily, and wanting to sleep a lot. She told me that she wasn't as interested in socializing and withdrew from the friends who were pushing her to share in the usual activities.

As long as Leigh stuck to concrete behaviors, she was pretty good at communicating. This was a good sign that with some help and guidance she would quickly learn to verbalize the internal emotions that were reflecting her pain. With an increase in emotional communication skills, she would then give herself the opportunity to understand these feelings. This would pave the way for growth and the creation of positive changes.

This client, entering therapy as a "Level Two", knew that she was hurting and even what it was all about, but she did not know how to talk about it or what steps to take to help herself. Her mother's suggestion of therapy was a little scary, as it was something new, but she was able to grasp the opportunity for help.

LEVEL THREE

- Can express most feelings.
- Needs some work identifying deeper, more compli-cated emotions.
- Willing to talk about feelings and emotions but usu-ally needs some skills to communicate effectively and in a healthy manner.
- Needs work in going beyond identification and ex-pression of emotions into creating positive changes.
- Usually seeks out therapy and is ready to work and grow.

Jane and Don sought marital therapy to recover from Don's extramarital affair. He had returned home, and they both knew that they had many prob-lems and issues to work out. Each was fairly adept at identifying and expressing feelings and at times even showed skillful communication techniques. Jane's tendency to take everything personally and respond with defensiveness and anger played right into Don's tendency to feel guilty and defensive. He would then feel resentful and irritated and would emotionally withdraw. This triggered Jane into her abandonment and betrayal issues. They had a de-structive pattern going that they needed help learn-ing to identify and change.

The couple's initial skills of identifying feelings and emotions, along with their openness and willingness to work hard, helped them tremendously. They quickly learned to identify the destructive pattern, and each owned personal issues that contributed to unhealthy coping styles.

Only a little bit of time was required to develop bonding and build trust in the therapeutic relationship, and they jumped at the opportunity to learn and practice new skills. They embraced change and openly discussed setbacks and old behaviors when they saw them.

LEVEL FOUR

- Good to excellent ability to identify feelings.
- Very open communication with many good skills, although, may need to learn more or fine tune existing techniques.
- Has usually made several attempts to create positive changes in a healthy manner but is frustrated by lack of progress.
- May need help in clarifying external issues as well as differentiating and owning personal ones.
- Personally seeks therapy when needed and is excited and eager to learn and grow.

Jeannie came back into therapy after having done a lot of hard work to progress through the first three therapy levels. When she started the first time, she had all the features of a "Level One" person. She had left therapy with a good grasp of the skills included in the "Level Four" description.

She was back to seek help in dealing with her marriage. Things had not fallen into a comfortable place with her husband. He had tolerated her self-

growth and resisted any of her attempts to engage him in his own process of self-discovery. The differences in their levels of functioning were becoming more of an issue.

Jeannie's husband was a hardworking, reliable individual and she respected him. He functioned at a "Level One" and sometimes a "Level Two" when he was forced to push his comfort zone in times of crisis. Jeannie was feeling increasingly lonely and frustrated, longing for him to learn to grow and share himself with her on a more intimate and developed level.

Jeannie realized that she needed assistance in dealing with the marital issues, so she reentered therapy to continue her own growth and development. We worked on identifying which were her issues and which were the things she perceived were her husband's. She learned to let go of "fixing him" and focus on herself. She quickly put her previously learned skills into practice and began to clarify her emotions and work on a healthy way to express these feelings to her husband. When he was unable to hear and understand her issues with him and refused to go with her to therapy to work things out, she reluctantly separated from him.

After several months Jeannie's husband called for an appointment. He was miserable and ready to do whatever was necessary to get her back. He began his process of working through the levels, reluctantly at first, but with more and more enthusiasm as he progressed in his growth and found out it really was an exciting thing to do.

LEVEL FIVE

- Excellent ability to identify feelings, both subtle and overt.
- Excellent ability to communicate effectively.
- Usually can create positive changes when a problem is identified and knows it is okay to seek help to achieve this.
- Usually enters into therapy requesting assistance regarding a specific problem. Sometimes a pattern of unhealthy behavior or emotions has been recognized. This can be seen as an opportunity to move beyond the unhealthy patterns into higher levels of personal and spiritual growth.

April, age 39, was grieving the death of both of her parents. They died within six months of each other from long term illnesses. She had felt prepared for them to die and had no regrets about her relationship with each of them. Old issues had long since been worked through, and she had a good relationship with both her mother and her father.

April decided she should seek therapy when the expected and understandable grief continued without letting up for about seven months. She began having a hard time functioning at work and with her family. She started her first session, clearly describing her feelings and behaviors. She elaborated on her thought processes and attempts at dealing with the feelings. Admitting her confusion and frustration regarding the lack of improvement in her grief and depression, she asked if I could help her see the things she was missing and move forward.

April and I explored her coping skills and personality traits. She was able to verbalize these and respond to my probing without defensiveness and fear. When we entered a vulnerable area, her feelings matched her behavior. For example, she cried and looked sad when talking about the funerals. She expressed feelings of anger and amazement after discovering that she never thought that her parents would die within six months of each other. She realized that she felt betrayed that things occurred that way and that she had been unconsciously holding onto that anger. These feelings were not acceptable to April on a conscious level as they felt "wrong and unfair." She had repressed them and unconsciously tried to force herself to feel differently -- the defense mechanism of "reaction formation." This confusion led to an increase in April's depression.

April also learned that she had expected herself to handle the grief of her parent's death as she had always done everything else in her life -- with efficiency, sensitivity, and determination. This awareness, along with her other hard work, was the turning point in her recovery.

April was able to recognize, actually remind herself, that she must grieve in her own time. Simply because she was taking longer than she thought was healthy, it needed to be okay. She had to examine her tendency to place extremely high expectations on herself and be somewhat critical if she fell short.

April had returned to her overly full life of career and family very quickly after the last funeral. Feel-

ing that she had allowed herself to take a lot of time off when each parent was dying and a few weeks to grieve and process her feelings, it had felt necessary to return to her life. She knew she needed to continue to grieve and was not afraid of the feelings. However, she inadvertently left no time in her schedule to do so.

April left therapy after about five sessions. She had taken the action necessary to let those around her know what she had learned and what she needed. She cut everything back to a level that she could handle and gave herself permission to grieve as long as it took. We made a plan for her to return to therapy if at any point she began worrying that she wasn't progressing toward recovery and acceptance.

PATTERNS OF BEHAVIOR

When you have recognized the "Emotional Growth Level" that you are working from, you will be on your way to discovering the patterns you use to cope with your life. These patterns tend to run in cycles of emotional responses and behaviors. People often get stuck in their own particular cycle. Only an effort to "lower the waterline" and raise the dynamics of their cycle of behavior to a conscious level will help them get unstuck.

AN UNHEALTHY PATTERN
OF BEHAVIOR

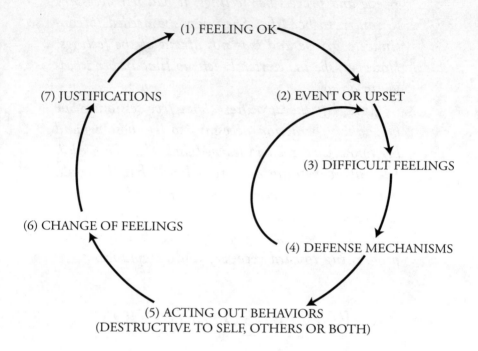

(1) FEELING OK

(7) JUSTIFICATIONS

(2) EVENT OR UPSET

(3) DIFFICULT FEELINGS

(6) CHANGE OF FEELINGS

(4) DEFENSE MECHANISMS

(5) ACTING OUT BEHAVIORS
(DESTRUCTIVE TO SELF, OTHERS OR BOTH)

Step one of this unhealthy cycle of behaviors is "feeling okay" about things at the moment or in general in your life. Step two takes us to an event or upset that occurs. This can be something small and seemingly insignificant to others, or it can be a catastrophic event that completely changes things. This upsetting event leads to difficult feelings (step three) which creates a crisis in the person who does not know how to identify or deal with these emotions. Unhealthy defense mechanisms are mobilized (step four) such as denial, blaming, isolation, withdrawal, or any of the many others.

At this point, after the defense mechanisms are in

action, a minicycle within the big cycle can develop. This minicycle fuels the feelings of victimization, resentment, anger, and fear along with all the other, yet unidentified, difficult feelings in step three. Eventually, to get unstuck from this nasty, vicious loop, a person breaks free by "acting out" (step five) with behaviors that are personally destructive or harmful to others or both.

Once the "acting out" occurs there can be a "change in feelings" (step six). These feelings may still be pretty hard to experience, but now they are at least different. The emotions are guilt, hurt, pain, embarrassment, or a multitude of other possibilities related to the "acting out." The "acting out" is something a person usually does to relieve the tension and anxiety caused by the difficult feelings created by the event or crisis. They usually have no idea how to identify or deal with those feelings, so they behave in some manner ("acting out") that creates a "change in feelings." These new feelings, the reaction to the "acting out," are usually more familiar and therefore much less frightening.

After a sufficient amount of time (which can vary tremendously) is spent wallowing in the different set of feelings in step six, the "justifications" (step seven) begin. At this step you rationalize, intellectualize, and justify why your acting out behavior was either fair, necessary, or not your fault. This enables you to come full circle and "feel okay" once more -- until the next event or crisis.

Jonathan, a 36-year-old construction worker, began therapy when his third marriage failed. He was very depressed, and it was only because he was in deep pain that he would even consider talking to a counselor. His "Emotional Growth Level" was in the first stage of development. He had virtually no skills in identifying or expressing any emotions other than depression and anger. He spent the first several sessions blaming his pain on his former wives, his parents, and the world. All three of Jonathan's marriages sounded very similar from their courtships to their traumatic, hostile endings. He had been unable to change any of his dysfunctional patterns of behavior. Jonathan's answer to this problem was to never fall in love again and never, ever get married again because "all women were like this and it would never work."

It took Jonathan quite awhile to begin to look at his own behaviors and emotions. Once he began to accept some personal responsibility, we were able to identify his dysfunctional cycle of behavior.

Jonathan recognized that when he was at a step one of "feeling okay," it did not take much of an event or crisis to really trigger him into his cycle. The "difficult emotions" of step three were so overwhelming and frightening to him that he withdrew into his shell and tried to pretend it would all go away. Whenever possible, he would put on a mask and deny that he was upset on the outside, all the while, churning inside with anxiety and unidentified feelings. His thoughts would turn to fantasies of revenge against whoever or whatever caused his upset. These unacceptable thoughts made Jonathan certain that he was as "bad and evil" as he had always suspected and only served to fuel his upset and subsequent "difficult emotions."

After a length of time, sometimes several hours and at times weeks or months, of stewing in his emotions and negative thoughts, Jonathan would reach a point where he could not stand it anymore. His acting out usually took the form of getting drunk and then unleashing all the horrible, angry thoughts and feelings that had been building up inside. He mostly directed this negative barrage at himself, but there were plenty of times it was aimed at whoever was around, which was usually his wife.

The day after an "acting out" episode, Jonathan would feel tremendously remorseful and guilty. He would also feel relieved that he had blown the tension out of his emotional bottle. He immediately launched into his justifications -- he had been under a lot of "tension and stress" and simply needed to "tie one on" to "let down his hair" and he was "really sorry, but it's over now" and "besides it wasn't my fault anyway." This allowed Jonathan to return to a state of "feeling okay."

With awareness and ownership of his dysfunctional cycle, Jonathan was finally able to see why all three of his wives left him. They all had told him, on their way out the door, that they were tired of his drinking, explosions, and excuses for his behavior. It became evident to each woman that Jonathan did not have any desire to change, so each, in turn, left him. Jonathan's newfound awareness that they had all been right was startling and very humbling. It was also the beginning of some really great therapeutic work on his part.

The place to break free from a dysfunctional cycle of behavior is at step three. This is the step where difficult feelings begin. You must learn to first identify and then deal with these difficult emotions that follow any event or crisis. It would be nice if we could change this cycle by stopping the upsetting events, and at times this is possible, but usually this is simply a part of life. ***Learning to effectively identify, handle, and communicate the difficult emotions that naturally go along with life's upsets are the keys to creating healthy patterns of behavior.***

One of the tools I give to people who are learning to identify and express their emotions is a "feeling sheet" (located at the end of this chapter). This is a list of many of the emotions we experience in response to both positive and negative events. Using the feeling sheet during or after a significant event can help put words to the jumble of emotions that can be experienced. Once these feelings are identified, it becomes easier to communicate them to someone else.

The feeling sheet is very simple to use. It works well to keep some at home, at work, in the car, in a purse, or briefcase. When a problem occurs, as soon as time allows, circle or highlight the pertaining feelings. When a person utilizes this process of identification for awhile, eventually a vocabulary of feeling words is established and the feeling sheet becomes unnecessary.

Developing the words to express how we feel inside is so important. First we must be able to know for ourselves how we feel. Only then can we begin to learn how to explain our feelings to another person. Good communication skills begin with the ability to express ourselves accurately and intelligently.

A healthy cycle of behavior involves many of the lessons you have already learned in Chapters One and Two. We all need to recognize that we have a tendency to view life's problems with Fear. The difficult emotions that are created by our fearful reactions make things even harder for us. "Bottling" the emotions and stuffing them in an attempt to deny and avoid them are like ignoring an infection and hoping it will go away. The ultimate explosion of "acting out" behavior simply creates more havoc and chaos which draws us down in one of those horrible, negative spirals.

Create an image of the healthy cycle for your response the next time life deals you a challenge. Knowing what it is you would like to achieve is an excellent step in making it happen. Here is an example of one healthy cycle of behavior. See if it fits for you.

A HEALTHY PATTERN
OF BEHAVIOR

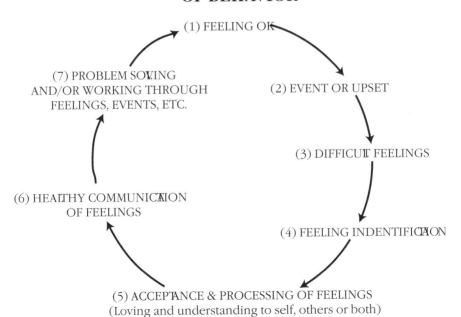

(1) FEELING OK

(2) EVENT OR UPSET

(3) DIFFICULT FEELINGS

(4) FEELING INDENTIFICATION

(5) ACCEPTANCE & PROCESSING OF FEELINGS
(Loving and understanding to self, others or both)

(6) HEALTHY COMMUNICATION OF FEELINGS

(7) PROBLEM SOLVING AND/OR WORKING THROUGH FEELINGS, EVENTS, ETC.

Working our way through the different levels of growth, whether they are "Trusting Levels" or "Emotional Growth Levels," can be scary and exciting, challenging or frustrating. The new insights about your behavior can even be a little overwhelming. Remember that there is not a set formula for the process of "self-growth." You cannot "do it wrong" or "mess it up." The only thing even close to messing it up is not trying to grow at all. Take all of this one step at a time and absorb whatever you can right now. You will surprise yourself, when you go back and read these chapters again at a later time, with how much you have learned and how far you have come in your growth.

FEELINGS SHEET

You may experience any of these feelings, but often fail to identify them specifically:

abandoned	charmed	deceitful	effeminate
absent-minded	cheated	defeated	egotistical
active	cheerful	defensive	electrified
adamant	childish	delighted	emotional
adaptable	civilized	demanding	empathic
adequate	clear-thinking	dependable	enchanted
adventurous	clever	depressed	energetic
affected	coarse	desirous	enraged
affectionate	cold	despondent	enterprising
aggressive	combative	destructive	enthusiastic
altered	commonplace	determined	envious
almighty	competitive	different	evasive
aloof	complaining	defiant	evil
ambitious	conceited	dignified	exasperated
ambivalent	condemned	diminished	excitable
angry	confident	disappointed	excited
annoyed	confused	discontented	exhausted
anxious	conspicuous	discreet	fair-minded
apathetic	conscientious	disorderly	fascinating
appreciative	conservative	dissatisfied	fearful
argumentative	considerate	distracted	feminine
arrogant	contented	distraught	flustered
artistic	contrite	distrustful	foolish
assertive	conventional	disturbed	forceful
astounded	cool	divided	foresighted
awed	cooperative	dominant	forgetful
awkward	courageous	dreamy	forgiving
bad	cowardly	dubious	formal
beautiful	cruel	dull	frank
betrayed	crushed	eager	frantic
bitter	curious	easygoing	free
blissful	cynical	ecstatic	friendly
changeable	daring	efficient	frightened

frivolous	immoral	low	overwhelmed
frustrated	impatient	loyal	pained
full	imposed upon	lustful	painstaking
fussy	impressed	mad	panicked
generous	independent	mannerly	parsimonious
gentle	indifferent	masculine	patient
glad	individualistic	mature	peaceful
gloomy	industrious	maudlin	peculiar
good	infantile	mean	persecuted
good-natured	infatuated	meek	preserving
gratified	informal	melancholy	persistent
greedy	infuriated	mild	pessimistic
groovy	inhibited	mischievous	petrified
guilty	inspired	miserable	pitiful
gullible	intelligent	moderate	pleasant
happy	intimate	modest	pleased
hard-headed	intolerant	moody	pleasure seeking
hasty	inventive	mystical	poised
headstrong	irresponsible	nagging	polished
heavenly	isolated	natural	practical
helpful	jealous	naughty	praising
helpless	jolly	ingenious	precarious
high	jumpy	nervous	precise
high-strung	keen	nice	prejudiced
homesick	kicky	noisy	pressured
honest	kind	nutty	pretty
honored	kinky	obliging	prim
horrible	laconic	obnoxious	prissy
hostile	lazy	obsessed	progressive
humorless	lecherous	odd	proud
humorous	left out	opposed	prudish
hurried	leisurely	optimistic	quarrelsome
hurt	licentious	opinionated	queer
hysterical	logical	organized	quit
idealistic	lonely	original	rational
ignored	longing	outgoing	rattlebrained
imaginative	loud	outraged	realistic
immature	loving	outspoken	reasonable

rebellious	sexy	stuffed	unassuming
reckless	shallow	stupid	undependable
reflective	sharp-witted	stunned	understanding
refreshed	shiftless	stupefied	uneasy
rejected	shocked	submissive	unemotional
relaxed	show-offish	suffering	unexcitable
reliable	shrewd	sulky	unfriendly
relieved	shy	superstitious	uninhibited
remorseful	silent	sure	unintelligent
resentful	silly	suspicious	unkind
reserved	simple	sympathetic	unrealistic
resourceful	sincere	tactful	unscrupulous
responsible	skeptical	tactless	unselfish
restless	slipshod	talkative	unsettled
retiring	slow	temperamental	unstable
reverent	sly	tempted	vehement
rewarded	smug	tenacious	versatile
righteous	sneaky	tense	vindictive
rigid	snobbish	tentative	violent
rude	sociable	terrible	vital
sad	softhearted	tenuous	vivacious
sarcastic	solemn	thankless	vulnerable
satisfied	sophisticated	thorough	warm
scared	sorrowful	thoughtful	wary
screwed up	spendthrift	threatened	weak
self-centered	spineless	thrifty	weepy
self-confident	spiteful	thwarted	whiny
self-controlled	spontaneous	timid	wholesome
self-denying	spunky	tired	wicked
self-punishing	stable	tolerant	withdrawn
self-seeking	startled	touchy	wise
selfish	steady	tough	witty
sensitive	stern	trapped	wonderful
sentimental	stingy	troubled	worried
serious	stolid	trusting	worrying
servile	strangled	ugly	zany
settled	strong	unaffected	
severe	stubborn	unambitious	

DEFENSE MECHANISMS

Look over the following descriptions of some of the most common defense mechanisms and see if you can find your usual repertoire of responses:

- ACTING OUT - giving into an impulse to behave in some manner to avoid feeling something;

- AVOIDANCE - staying away from or "avoiding" looking at or dealing with something or someone;

- BLAMING - assigning responsibility to someone or something besides yourself;

- CONTROLLING - excessive attempts to manage or regulate events in one's environment to minimize anxiety and to resolve inner conflicts;

- DENIAL - a tendency to ignore aspects of reality;

- DISPLACEMENT - shifting feelings to another person, object, or idea that resembles the original to some degree;

- EXCESSIVE HUMOR - excessive use of sarcasm, wit, or humor to displace, deny, sexualize, or avoid feelings;

- INTELLECTUALIZATION - excessive use of intellectual processes to avoid feelings and emotions;

- ISOLATION / WITHDRAWAL - remaining aloof and separate from others;

- PROJECTION - assuming that others feel the same way you do - projecting your feelings, thoughts, or opinions onto another;

- RATIONALIZATION - rational explanations used in an attempt to justify or "rationalize" a feeling, thought, or behavior that would otherwise be unacceptable;

- REGRESSION - attempting to return to an earlier phase of development and functioning to avoid the feelings at the present level of development;

- REPRESSION - a conscious or unconscious attempt to "shove under" feelings, thoughts, beliefs, events, and/or behaviors from conscious awareness;

- REACTION FORMATION - first a repression of unwanted thoughts or beliefs, then compulsively striving to think, feel, or behave the opposite;

- SEXUALIZATION - giving a person, object, or event sexual significance that it would not otherwise have in order to handle feelings.

ATTITUDE

The longer I live, the more I realize the impact of attitude on life.

Attitude, to me, is more important than facts. It is more than the past, than education, than circumstances, than failure, than successes, than what other people think or say or do.

It is more important than appearance, giftedness or skill. It will make or break a company, a church, a home.

The remarkable thing is we have a choice every day regarding the attitude we will embrace for that day.

We cannot change the inevitable. The only thing we can do is play on the one string we have, and that is our attitude.

I am convinced that life is ten percent what happens to me and ninety percent how I react to it.

And so it is with you...

-- Charles Swindoll

CHAPTER FOUR

TAKING RISKS

*"You are always being
given opportunities
to love and be loved,
yet ask yourself how many
times in your life you have
squandered these opportunities."
-- Gary Zukav*

"I wasn't planning on stealing the makeup," explained 15-year-old Jenny. "I even had money with me. My friend and I were just looking at the lipsticks and joking around. She dared me to rip one off, and I guess I thought it would be kind of fun."

"What did you think would happen if you got caught?" I inquired.

"I didn't think about that. I mean, I didn't think I'd get caught. I don't know what I was thinking. It just sort of happened." Jenny spoke with a sullen, exasperated look on her face as she slumped low in the glide rocking chair in my office. The toe of her expensive tennis shoe pushed casually against the corner of the table and made her slide gently back and forth in the rocker. A wisp of light brown hair fell over her hazel eyes.

I watched her for a few moments and finally broke the silence. "Do you always take risks without thinking about the consequences?" I asked, trying not to sound like a parent.

"No. I mean, yes. I mean...what?"

"Consequences. The things that happen as a re-action to something we do. Sometimes they're good and sometimes they're pretty painful. What was the consequence for getting caught shoplifting?"

Jenny bolted straight up in the chair and ex-claimed, "You should have seen that security guard. He grabbed my arm and said, 'Can you empty your pockets for me, young lady.' I just about, well...messed my pants, he was scary. I started shaking and cry-ing. He took me back inside and called the police. Then they called my parents. Both of them came down to the store. My dad had to leave an important meeting to come. My mom had that look on her face. I hate that look. All I could think about was how stupid I was. The store charged my parents a $250.00 fine, and I have to earn the money to pay them back. We have an appointment at the police station next week to talk to some juvenile officer. Do you think they're going to put me in Juvenile Hall? Everyone kept saying that now I'd have a record. This whole thing really sucks. Then they made this appointment with you because my mom and dad said something must be really wrong with me. Do you think I'm mentally ill?" Jenny tumbled all of it out without any noticeable breaths.

I waited for Jenny to catch her breath and calmly replied, "You've asked a lot of good questions that we need to be sure to address. First, let's take a look at the whole idea of taking risks."

THE SAFE ZONE

In order to take a risk you have to step outside of a place that has not been risky for you. Let's call that place the "SAFE ZONE." The Safe Zone is a calmer place where you know what the expectations are. Sometimes the Safe Zone is lonely and boring as well as safe.

When you are presented with a challenge, opportunity, or adventure, you have to step outside of the Safe Zone to take the "RISK" of going for it. A risk can be anything from a simple thing like daring to tell a joke or speaking in front of the class to a big challenge like allowing yourself to try a new relationship or leaving an existing, bad relationship. Some risks we usually decide not to take at all. Would you take the risk of walking a high wire stretched across the Grand Canyon? Most could say no to that one without much hesitation.

SAFE ZONE   - - - - - - - - - - - - - - - - **RISK**

• *Known expectations*
• *Predictable*
• *Can get boring*
• *Can be lonely*

"Can you tell me what your Safe Zone was just before you took the Risk to shoplift?" I asked Jenny.

Jenny thought about my question while she rocked the chair a few more times. "I guess my Safe Zone was there when my friend and I were just walking around the mall looking at stuff. We were talking and checking out the guys and looking at clothes. The regular old junk we do when we go to the mall."

"Was it boring?"

"No. We like to go to the mall and do that stuff. We don't do anything to get in trouble...well, we never have before. We just hang out. It's not really boring."

"So, when you hang out at the mall, you know what's expected of you?"

"How could I forget. My mom drops us off and gives us lecture number 256. You know, 'Be polite, don't leave the mall premises, don't talk to strangers, meet me at the J.C. Penney's entrance at exactly three o'clock, don't be late, etc., etc., etc.,'" Jenny reiterated, with one of those looks that only a 15- year-old can muster.

"Can you tell me the exact moment that the "RISK" of taking the lipstick came into your mind?"

"Kim, my friend, said that the color looked cool on me and suggested I buy it. I said I didn't want to blow my allowance on makeup because I already have some. Kim said, 'Just take it. Put it in your pocket. No one will see.' I didn't really want to. I mean, I know stealing is wrong, but the idea of it was also kind of exciting. I just did it real quick. I stuck it in my pocket and walked around the store *some more. My heart was pounding and I felt weird. We walked out of the store and that's when the guy grabbed my arm. I never thought of stealing the lipstick as taking a risk."*

"You were doing okay in the Safe Zone and then you jumped into taking a Risk. Did you stop to think about the consequences of the risk you were taking?"

Her toe gave a hard push on the table and the chair jumped back. "No."

Whenever we take a risk, no matter how large or small, there are consequences. Sometimes the consequences are positive, sometimes negative, and occasionally a little of each. When I take a risk, I like to say to myself, "What's the worst that can happen?" If the outcome is obviously negative, like my high wire example, I'll probably decide immediately not to take the risk. Most of the time the consequences are subtle, and we have to weigh the possible outcomes more slowly.

"Let's pretend that you're back in the store and you're looking at the possible consequences of the risk you're considering. Tell me what the most positive outcome could be."

"I'd get the lipstick for free and not have to spend my allowance," Jenny quipped immediately.

"Okay. That would feel good?" I asked.

"Yeah. Maybe. I probably would have felt guilty about it later. I'd have to hide it from my mom because she'd ask how much it cost, and then if she saw I still had my allowance, she'd get suspicious."

"So even your best outcome would have had some

negative consequences. Tell me about the worst case scenario."

"Well, I guess if I had thought about it I could have figured out what would happen if I got caught. I've heard of some kids at school getting busted for shoplifting, so I sort of know what they do to you. I could have pictured that look my mom would get on her face and that would have been enough to stop me," she giggled briefly and immediately became serious again. Jenny's eyes teared up and she stared solemnly at her hands folded in her lap.

Stopping to weigh the consequences of a potential risk is a good thing to do, but not something everyone always does. Teenagers are notorious for just stepping blindly into a risk and then paying for it later. Think of all the risks a teenager faces on almost a daily basis -- standing up in class, talking to a new person, or wearing something different. Big risks like drugs, alcohol, cigarettes, sex, relationships, driving, and many more are there on a constant basis.

Many adults do not stop to think what could happen if they risk certain behaviors. Think of the multitude of challenges that are presented on a daily basis. Most of them are weighed consciously or unconsciously, a decision is made, and the risk is either taken or abandoned. Let's look at some of the positive and negative outcomes that can happen to any type of risk.

POSITIVE OUTCOMES *NEGATIVE OUTCOMES*

POSITIVE OUTCOMES	NEGATIVE OUTCOMES
Love	Rejection
Joy	Depression
Pleasure	Pain
Success	Failure
Acceptance	Loss
Financial Gain	Financial Loss
Companionship	Loneliness
Freedom	Imprisonment
Increased self-esteem	Lowered self-esteem
	Illness
	Death

If we keep the entire picture in our mind of what healthy risk taking looks like, we have a better chance of making the types of decisions that will honor ourselves and others.

TAKING RISKS

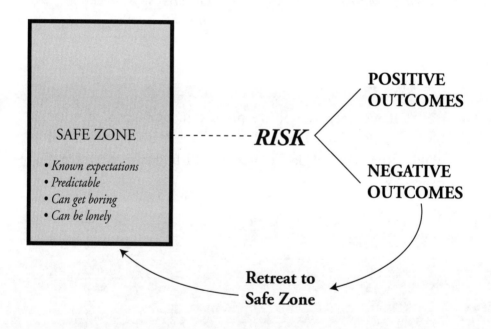

Bob and his wife, Barbara, entered into therapy to try to fix a deteriorating, 23-year marriage. Both agreed they had been unhappy for the past 15 years. After a great deal of hard work on communication skills, trusting abilities, working through old hurts, and anger, they came to the conclusion that they simply were not right for each other. They had grown apart, the attraction had died, and they did not want to stay together simply because it was expected of them by their grown children. We worked on the skills on how to separate amicably, and they did a lot of talking about staying friends.

After awhile it became apparent that Bob and Barbara could talk about separating but actually diving in and taking the risk of changing everything was very frightening. For awhile they thought it must mean they were still in love with each other, so they tried again to work things out. They kept coming back to wanting to be apart but being afraid of taking the risk.

There were many wonderful therapeutic opportunities during Bob and Barbara's period of indecision. We worked on healthy, decision-making techniques, dealing with change, creating positive outcomes, and healthy, risk-taking skills.

They eventually took the plunge and separated. It was very difficult for both of them emotionally and financially. They used their communication skills to help their adult children through the grief of a family breakup. Now, five years later, Bob has remarried and is very happy. He obviously used his many new skills to choose a healthy partner and has worked to keep his relationship open and growing. Barbara threw herself into her career and has really made a name for herself. She hopes to find a satisfying relationship some day but is okay with it happening in its own time. Bob and Barbara have remained friends and do well at family gatherings when they're together.

Taking risks is not a simple thing nor something that should be taken lightly. The more you learn to weigh the consequences and develop healthy skills, the better you become at taking appropriate risks and creating more positive outcomes.

Living in an era with a constant stream of new technology has provided many creative and unusual opportunities for risks in our lives. One of the most powerful, interesting, and intimidating innovations to be introduced in a long time is the Internet. This system uses the vast resources of computer technology to give access to anyone with a computer, a modem (an internal computer/telephone connection), and a telephone line, the ability to "log on" and surf the computer information highways. A person can talk to someone across the world or down the block simply by typing messages on the screen and hitting a key to send them on their way. From the comfort of home, it is possible to do extensive research and share findings with other people in your field of interest. The possibilities are endless -- so are the risks.

People are faced with risks when accessing the superhighway of computer technology. As it is with all risks, there are good things to be gleaned and lessons to be learned from this newest form of relationship interactions.

Judy was lonely and bored when she began playing around with the computer that she and her husband had bought for the kid's schoolwork. At 46 years old, with two teenagers, Judy was beginning to feel useless, undirected, and dull. She had left her career as a dental assistant when she married Dan, 23 years ago. The idea of going back to college seemed overwhelming, but the thought of taking a minimum wage job simply to stay busy did not thrill Judy either. She felt lost -- until her son showed her how to log onto the Internet.

Judy was intimidated by the computer at first. However, she quickly became adept at "surfing the web," entering "chat rooms," helping her kids research school papers, and even printing out papers on engineering for her husband and his work. She didn't worry about looking "old and frumpy," as she called herself. She could be herself and not feel shy. Judy made many friends "on-line" and began to spend more and more of her time sitting in front of the computer screen tapping out messages to send in her back-and-forth conversations.

Dan was relieved, at first, with Judy's newfound interest in the computer. It kept her busy and off his back. She stopped harassing him about coming home from work and plopping down in his favorite chair with a beer to watch the news. Now when he fell asleep in front of the television after dinner, she did not even notice because she was busy in the den with the computer. In fact, more often than not, it would be Dan who would wake himself by snoring too loudly, get out of his chair, and find her, still wide awake, in the den. He'd tell her it was late, sometimes one or two or three o'clock in the morning, and ask her if she was coming to bed. Judy's usual reply was "in a minute." On several occasions Dan rose to his alarm clock only to find Judy still in front of the computer -- she had stayed up all night talking to friends.

When Judy called for an appointment for therapy, Dan was supportive. He felt that she was "addicted" to the computer and that it was ruining their relationship. During Judy's first session, she cried and said that their relationship had been nothing but an empty shell for a long time. She was not going to give up the newfound meaning and purpose she had finally found in her life. Judy wanted to come to therapy because she had fallen in love with a 28-year-old man she had met on-line. She was frightened because she found herself considering giving up her marriage and family to move across the country to be with him.

Judy had entered into an arena that was so new that she did not have a set of values, morals, or experiences to guide her in how to handle this type of risk. She was a woman of high moral standards and good values and would never have considered having an affair. Talking, albeit extremely intimately, over the computer, did not seem to violate any of the rules of conduct that she had been taught. She had even told Dan about her on-line friends, leaving out, of course, the ever increasing intimacy with this one man.

Judy tried to justify the uneasiness she felt about this new "friendship" by telling herself she wasn't doing anything wrong. How could you do anything improper while sitting in your own home, 3,000 miles away, with your husband sawing logs in front of the television in the next room? It must be safe -- but was it?

Simply because something, like the Internet, is new does not mean we need to avoid exploring the opportunities. As in any choice to go outside the "safe zone," we must weigh the risks involved and move cautiously should we decide to go for it. Listening to that "little voice inside" can be very helpful in assessing our progress. If Judy had listened to herself, she would have known she was venturing into dangerous territory.

As it turned out with Judy and Dan, she did leave the marriage. She told Dan she was in love with this man she had never met in person, packed a suitcase, and flew across the country to move in with him. After two weeks Judy realized that she had made a terrible mistake. This man, although nice, had many problems and was hoping that she would "take care of him."

During the time Judy was gone, Dan, in horrible pain, came into therapy to try to make sense of it all. It was an opportunity for him to look at himself. When Judy returned, they entered into marital therapy together and continued to work on their individual self-growth issues as well. Of course, there was also a lot of healing that needed to be done surrounding this "affair" and Judy's willingness to abandon the marriage and Dan. Each grew tremendously from this experience but would quickly say they would rather have found an easier way to make it all come about.

While any risk, whether it yield positive or negative consequences, can lead to the opportunity for self-growth, it is wise to learn to risk intelligently. Sometimes we can achieve the same opportunity for growth, with a lot less pain and agony, if we only weigh the potential consequences before we act. If we take the time to look ahead to the outcome we are trying to achieve, maybe we can see an easier way to get there.

Robert, age 53, entered therapy to deal with the sexual molestation that occurred when he was 9 years old. A 16-year-old babysitter had repeatedly molested him over the course of a year. He had never told anyone about this until he spoke to an unknown, unseen man on the Internet in a chat room for sexual abuse survivors. The man had encouraged him to seek therapy.

Robert had been using the computer through his work for e-mail messages from the home office across the country. He bought a computer for his home and began researching information on topics that interested him. Finally, Robert began to research the subject that he had wanted to know about for approximately four years -- his increasing problems with sex, specifically his inability to achieve or maintain an erection during love-making with his wife.

Talking to his family doctor had proven embarrassing and unproductive for Robert. He only did it at his wife's insistence to rule out some possible physical problem. The doctor had told him that he was fine and this type of thing happened occasionally to men Robert's age. He said things would probably improve if Robert tried not to worry about it.

Robert began researching sexual problems over the Internet and learned that there were often psychological reasons behind these types of issues. He read several accounts of men, as well as women, molested as children, who subsequently experienced sexual difficulties.

The question Robert couldn't answer over the Internet was why this problem waited so long to surface in his life. His willingness to risk sharing in the chat room on the Internet gave him the push he needed to reach out for help. It only took about 30 minutes, in the first session, for the reason to become apparent. (Wouldn't it be great if it were always that easy?!)

When he sat down in my office, Robert had launched nervously into the facts surrounding the molestation he endured silently as a child. I asked him to tell me a little bit about his life now, and he told me about his wife and two children. When he mentioned that his oldest daughter was 20 and his son was 13 years old, I made a mental note. Four years ago, when Robert's sexual problems started, his children were the same age as Robert and his babysitter.

I asked Robert if he felt the age of his children

when his problems started had any significance. He
sat there stunned. Sometimes an awareness can hit
between the eyeballs and touch a core place inside
that lets you know "that's it!"

It turned out that Robert's repressed memories had
been triggered by the similar age characteristics of
his kids. These thoughts, especially in association with
his children, were reprehensible to him. He unconsciously used the defense mechanism of "reaction
formation" to try to keep himself from feeling any
sexual feelings -- positive or negative.

Robert's willingness to risk exploring his problem
on the Internet, along with his courage to seek help,
led to a complete cure of his sexual dysfunction and
a freedom from years of unconscious, internal torment about the molestation. In a few hours spent
on-line and three therapy sessions, Robert felt like "a
new man."

Learning to risk appropriately is not always an easy
task. There are a few simple steps to remember when facing an opportunity to risk:

1.   NOTICE - Know when you are about to take a risk.
      (Notice while you are still in the "safe zone", if pos-
      sible.)

2.   DEFINE IT - Define the risk.

3.   NEGATIVE OUTCOMES - Take the time to list the
      potential negative outcomes and ask yourself if you
      could live with them should they occur.

4. POSITIVE OUTCOMES - List potential positive outcomes. Would these be okay? What fears do they bring up for you?

5. BUY TIME - If you are being rushed into a decision, "buy time" to think about it. Tell the person you'll get back to them, ask for a few minutes to think, or even say you need to go to the restroom -- anything to give yourself the time you need to weigh the potential consequences.

6. AIM FOR THE POSITIVE - Should you decide to go ahead and take the risk, aim for the positive outcomes -- believe they can happen. Of course, keep your eyes and ears open for unforeseen consequences, but try to enjoy the adventure.

7. LEARN FROM IT - Whatever the outcome, learn the lessons that have been offered. Even if you totally blow it and do something really stupid, all is not lost if you allow yourself to grow from the experience. Remember, there are no failures, only lessons not yet learned.

THE SERENITY PRAYER

God grant me the serenity
to accept the things I cannot change,

Courage to change the things I can,

And wisdom to know the difference.

-- Reinhold Niebuhr (1892-1971)

CHAPTER FIVE

SIMPLIFYING – DEALING WITH STRESS

"The only way you can eliminate a bad habit is when it's standing in the way of something you want more."
-- Gandhi

Life often feels much too full. We struggle through our daily routines and agonize how to get it all done. Life is like laundry -- if you can ever reach a point where you think you have it all washed, folded, and put away, someone gets something dirty and throws it in the hamper. The whole cycle then starts all over again.

I call the phenomenon of trying to squeeze everything we have to do into a limited time schedule, *"TEN POUNDS OF JUNK IN A THREE POUND BAG"* or simply a "TEN IN THREE" for short. This is a phrase I use often, although I must admit, I don't always use the word "junk." Most people I know can function pretty well up to a "seven in three" (seven pounds of junk in their three pound bag); however, once they begin to go over seven, they start to "stress out." It's a little sad that we as a society have begun to accept a "seven in three" as normal and a "ten in three" as extremely common.

People can get creative in their attempts to deal with their stress. Sometimes these ingenious methods work; sometimes they do not. Occasionally they work for awhile and then stop being effective. Often, people whine about their stress but are not willing to do anything to change their situation. There is almost a sense of pride that their three pound bag is overflowing on a regular basis.

"I am on maximum overload. I just can't do this anymore. It is killing me," Jean said with a tone that was somewhere between a whine and an announcement. "You call this a 'ten in three,' Patty, but I think it's become fifteen pounds of crap in my three pound bag."

"Tell me what's going on," I said, trying not to sound impatient. I had heard some version of this statement on a weekly basis for the past month that I had been doing therapy with Jean, a 38-year-old mother of three with a full-time job.

For five minutes Jean rambled on about work, laundry, dishes, bills to pay, weeds in the garden, soccer practices, and her husband, John, who did not help enough. I knew from our past sessions that until Jean had a few minutes to vent her frustrations, she would not be ready to get down to the business of doing therapy.

Jean had a pattern of overloading herself and then blaming everyone around her for the stress it caused. Her anger and frustration became more and more intense as the stress built.

As Jean detailed her week to me, I found myself picturing a volcano filling up with hot, molten lava. The pressure had again built up until, by the end of the week, Jean was ready to blow. She did blow, of course, unloading all over John and the kids. When the explosion was over, she was again, remorseful and depressed. This was the pattern that had brought Jean into therapy in the first place.

"I've been working on taking responsibility for how my life operates, like we've talked about," Jean announced abruptly, as if she had finally heard the blaming quality of her monologue. "I'm beginning to see that I really do this to myself!"

"Hallelujah!!!!" I cried inside of my head. "That's a great awareness, Jean," I said aloud. "Taking responsibility for your life allows you to take back your personal power to begin to change things."

Each of us tends to have a certain amount of **"coping space"** available within ourselves to deal with daily life. **"Coping"** is our attempt to effectively deal with the trials and tribulations of our lives. The amount of stress we can handle, or how much "coping space" we have, varies between individuals. Some people naturally have more patience and ability to handle greater amounts of pressure. Some also seem to have superior skills to deal with life's stress. Fortunately, coping skills can be taught to those who have not had the opportunity to learn them. Also, the amount of coping space we have can be maximized by learning some simple techniques for identifying stress, dealing with it, and letting it go.

I use a visual image of a bottle that sits inside our torso to represent the amount of coping space each of us has. The neck of the bottle is located in our chest. The top, complete with a cork to hold in the contents, is sitting around our throat area. The base of the bottle, fuller and heavier, sits in our gut. The size of this internal bottle is not universal. Some people have a bigger bottle than others. The size of the bottle represents how much coping space we have.

There is no such thing as a totally empty bottle. Even the most high-functioning, well-adjusted people I have seen in therapy have something in their bottles. The stuff in the bottom of the bottle is called "life." "Life" can be made up of old childhood issues, past traumas, hurts, and events that tend to stay with us. They are not necessarily in our daily, conscious awareness, but we usually know that they are there.

People who have had difficult, traumatic childhoods would have more "life" issues in their bottles than those whose childhoods were less eventful. For example, a victim of sexual molestation might have a bottle that is half-full with "life" issues. This would leave only half of a bottle to cope with current situations. This person could enter into therapy to deal with these old issues and become a molest survivor. This would lessen the amount of room these old issues occupy in the bottle which would increase the amount of emotional and physical energy available for coping with life.

The amount of room left in your bottle after your "life" issues take up their chunk is called **"coping space."** When my client, Jean, told me that she couldn't take it anymore, she was telling me that her **"bottle was full."** People deal differently with a full bottle. Some leak around the edges of their cork and cry easily or are irritated and anger quickly. Some people, like Jean, hold the pressure inside until they explode like a volcano all over everyone.

"Exploders," the volcano-erupting type of people,

are seldom fair about when, how, and on whom they explode. They usually do a thing that I call **"last in -- first out."** The thing that makes them upset is rarely representative of the rest of the emotional junk in the bottle, but it is always the first thing that flies out of their exploding bottle.

For example: your bottle is full from a hard day at work, laundry that needs to be done, a fight with your spouse that morning -- not to mention the old "life" issues you've never dealt with -- and a multitude of little things. Your child comes up to you and asks when dinner will be ready, and you explode all over the place. You start hollering about fixing dinner, the laundry, and work. Your child stands there feeling covered with your foul, nasty stuff. Think of those old clichés, "the straw that broke the camel's back" and "the kick the dog" syndrome. Both sayings would fit with this bottle analogy.

"Leakers" are the people that try to alleviate the pressure of an overly full bottle by letting a little bit escape at a time as they leak around the edge of their corks. They seem easily irritated and often depressed and overwhelmed. Sometimes they seem to be whining and at other times are sharp and sarcastic.

In an effort to help cope with the pressure, both "leakers" and "exploders" have a tendency to use any method at their disposal to keep their corks down. Some of these methods of coping are healthier than others. Exercise and hobbies can help distract from a full bottle. Drugs, alcohol, cigarettes, sexual addictions, and workaholic tendencies can seem to relieve pressure at first but actually add to the emotional turmoil in the long run. Any method used to distract attention from a full bottle becomes just that, a distraction. It does not change how full the bottle is or alter the contents. To truly lower your stress level you must reduce the contents of your bottle.

The most effective way to deal with stress is not just to "cope with it" but to learn how to alleviate as many of the stressful things as you can. Learning to identify -- **awareness** of what is in your bottle -- is the first step toward freeing yourself of the stressful contents.

Start by drawing your bottle on a piece of paper. You don't have to be a great artist. Just make a little sketch. Now mark off how much room you think your "life" issues take up in your bottle. This is a subjective type of self-evaluation that may change as you become more familiar with just how much coping space you really do have in your bottle. If your old, life issues seem to be in your conscious awareness much of the time, then they probably occupy a good deal of space in your bottle. Conversely, if you do not have any major traumatic issues in your past, or if you have sufficiently worked through those that did occur, then your life issues may not take up a whole lot of room.

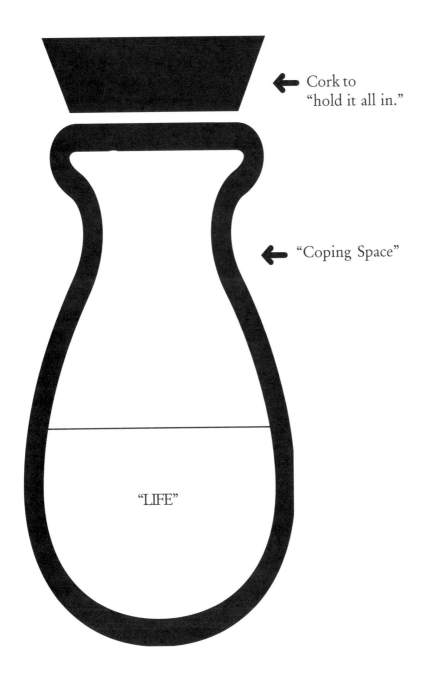

Cork to
"hold it all in."

"Coping Space"

"LIFE"

After you have allowed for your life issues, the amount of space left in your bottle is your "coping space." Now think about the major areas of stress in your life and portion out an amount of space that feels like it corresponds to that issue.

A typical example of a completed bottle might be:

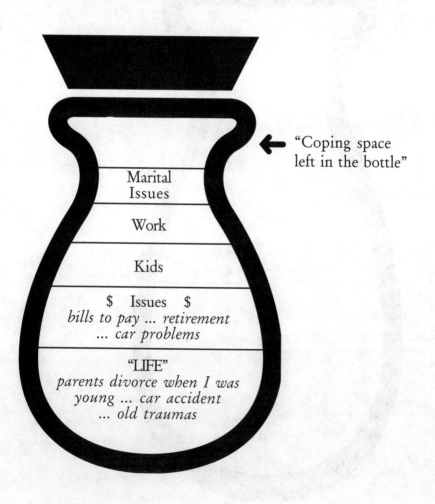

← "Coping space left in the bottle"

Marital Issues

Work

Kids

$ Issues $
bills to pay ... retirement ... car problems

"LIFE"
parents divorce when I was young ... car accident ... old traumas

How close to the top of your bottle do you feel you are right this minute? How close are you most of the time? What do you do when your bottle is full? Are you an "exploder" or a "leaker?" Does your bottle fill up quickly or slowly? What does it take to make you feel as though you've regained some coping space in your bottle?

If you feel like there simply is not enough room in this bottle drawing to enter all the areas that are pressuring you, then your bottle is most likely very full. This probably isn't earth shattering news to you. Admitting that we are stressed is fairly easy for most of us. In fact, at times, being stressed seems to be a status symbol suggesting that we are successful, popular, or very involved in life. It is common to hear someone brag about their outrageously high score on some magazine stress test.

The interesting part of it all is that most people talk about their full bottles as though someone else has filled them. There is a "victim" mentality when it comes to acknowledging the struggles of a full bottle. It's the kids or the boss or the bill collectors that are stressing them out. Many people tend to fill their lives beyond capacity and then wonder why their emotional coping bottles overflow as well.

"If I can just keep up this pace for a few more years, the mortgage will be paid off and then I can slow down a little. Maybe then things won't be so tough," Savannah justified. This was one of her calmer moments when she had lots of coping space in her bottle. A lot of coping space for Savannah means at least one quarter of an inch of space.

"Your willingness to live your life totally 'maxed

out' at all times blows me away," I told her for the one-hundredth time. I could talk to Savannah like that because she's my buddy, not my client. "Okay, so you'll get the stupid mortgage paid off, but you'll be dead by 50-years-old doing it." I gave her that look that said you know what I'm talking about.

Savannah laughed and immediately looked at the lifeline in her right hand. "Do you think it's grown any?" she asked with a twinkle in her eye as she stuck her hand an inch from my nose.

She was referring to a palm reading that she had several years ago when we went to a conference together. The reader, a wise and revered Japanese man, had told her that if she didn't significantly change her lifestyle immediately, she would be dead by fifty. Since then we have alternately joked about it and looked seriously at the wisdom of those words.

Savannah did begin to look at her harried, stressful lifestyle and made some significant changes. She changed her eating habits and began to exercise regularly. She made an effort to learn how to meditate and began to consider her spiritual growth an important part of her life. Sometimes I tell her that the "croak zone" must to be up to at least 53 or 54 with these changes. She knows that I keep pushing her to simplify even more.

Every time Savannah gets one quarter of an inch of room in her bottle she adds something else. She is a profoundly intelligent, extremely motivated, professional woman with three active children on top of all of that. One time we counted the number of scheduled places she went in one week and came up with

14 destinations. This included lessons, sports prac-
tices, and meetings. It did not include work related
activities, groceries, errands, trips to drop off kids at
friends' houses, or any of the other necessities it takes
to run a business or household.

Savannah's busy life is not much different from mine
or many other families of the 90's. Hers may be more intense than most, but it is an extremely common practice for
people to overload their lives with an assortment of activities that start out being fun but end up being stressful.

A good name for the things in life that we want to do
is **"wanna-do's"** and the things in life that we have to do is
"gotta-do's." The things that end up filling our bottles and
robbing us of our precious coping space tend to be the
"gotta-do's" not the "wanna-do's." A responsible, well-orga-
nized person will usually do their "gotta-do's" before their
"wanna-do's" in order to get them out of the way. In fact,
this is a coping skill that is useful to adults and children to
help them reduce their stress and allow them to relax.

If we take the time to do our "gotta-do's," we take
the worry and concern out of our bottles regarding those
issues. This leaves more coping space along with a feeling
of reduced pressure and gives us the ability to relax and
enjoy ourselves. Let kids know that if they do their homework and chores first, then they can do their fun things.
They know that they can get involved without having to
stop to do some "gotta-do." There is a pressured feeling to
your fun time if you know there is something hanging over
your head waiting to be done.

"GOTTA-DO'S BEFORE WANNA-DO'S" is a catchy
little phrase that can help keep the focus on getting things

done in order to create the space needed to truly relax. This concept is for those who struggle with procrastination but are now ready to create a healthier habit. Getting your responsibilities out of the way before beginning the things you want to do helps tremendously. The key to being ready to make the change is that you **"GOTTA WANNA."**

One of the biggest problems in dealing with stress is an overly full bottle. The bottle can be too full due to emotional issues that need to be worked out or from the responsibility of too many "gotta-do's" or both.

Many families today are stressed by too many obligations outside the home. It is common for both parents to work or for the household to be run by a single, working parent. Besides work, school, and home duties, there are often sports practices, lessons, and social obligations. Where is the downtime? If almost every day and evening is programmed with what becomes a series of "gotta-do's," when does a family relax with spontaneous, unplanned time? For many "stressed out" adults and children the answer is "almost never."

Twenty to thirty years ago there was not the pressure to compete that exists in today's world. Two parent homes with a working father and a stay-at-home mother were the norm. Children went to school and came home afterwards. When their homework was finished, they went out to play with the neighborhood children. If there were sports activities or band practice, they were usually after school on the school grounds, and the kids came home when practice was over. Some, not all, of the kids took music lessons or a dance class, but a child was not unusual if this was not the case. The teenagers that received the lead in the high school musicals were usually the ones with natural singing voices.

Life was simpler, less hectic, and less stressful.

Today we need two-income families, not only because the cost of living has risen so high, but also because expectations of ourselves, our children, and each other have risen to monstrous proportions. It is not unusual for parents to choose preschools based on the advanced curriculum capable of creating superachieving kindergartners. Music, dance, singing, and sports training begin earlier and earlier so that the children will be able to compete for the positions that will create the most opportunities. All of these extra activities cost a lot of money and take a lot of time to accomplish.

When a high school today has auditions for the lead in the musical, many of the adolescents competing for the parts have already had years of voice and acting lessons. Families spend significant amounts of time and money to acquire the latest, greatest computers and other electronic equipment. The people who cannot afford these luxuries find that their children may not be at a competitive level with other children their age.

It says a lot that the standard for an excellent report at many schools from sixth grade on up is now a typed, spell-checked, grammar-checked, computer-graphic-decorated, four-color-printed document. The pressure is becoming tremendous -- the pressure to compete, to succeed, and to simply "get by." Progress and competition can be wonderful things for our society. However, from a point of view of stress these improvements can send us off the scale in a stress test. The time, money, and effort that is required to compete in today's educational system in order to feel prepared for tomorrow's job market is incredible. I see more and more adolescents in therapy who sound like 55-year-old adults wishing they could retire. These kids are burned out by 15 or 16 and have their own versions of "nervous breakdowns" from the tremendous stress they are under.

It is impossible to create healthy coping skills to deal with stress if there are ten pounds of "stuff" in the three pound bag. Making the bag significantly bigger is not really an option either. Some people can stretch their comfort zones to try to make their bag a four pounder, but it is not easy to do. The answer lies in trying to relinquish the extra seven pounds of "stuff."

Have you ever cleaned out your garage or closets with the intention of disposing of everything you don't use? It's really hard to do. Trying to rid yourself of the extra seven pounds of "stuff" is a similar task. You must really want to do it ("gotta wanna") and stay really focused the entire time.

Emptying your bottle and fitting your life into your three pound bag are called "simplifying." In order to simplify you have to be aware of everything you are responsible for in your life. Think of some of the following areas as you make your list:

- Look at the keys on your key ring. Each one represents something or someone for which you are responsible.
- Take a look at your calendar and note all the places you must be at specific times. If you are responsible for others, like your children, add their schedules to yours.
- List your financial obligations.
- List committees, boards, and other time-consuming volunteer activities.

- List your responsibilities for daily, weekly, monthly and yearly chores and/or obligations such as holidays, birthdays, anniversaries, etc.
- Examine your exercise commitments.
- Chart out a typical 24-hour day in your life.

Becoming aware of what is in your bottle is actually the first step in simplifying your life. Simplifying is what empties the bottle and helps you to make your life a little easier. Wouldn't it be great to have a "five in three" instead of a "ten in three?" Here are the steps for emptying your bottle and simplifying your life:

EMPTYING YOUR BOTTLE

Step One: Awareness—Become aware of just what things are in your bottle. How much room do your life issues take up and what are the current issues with which you are struggling?

Step Two: Get rid of stuff—Tackle some of the simpler items you've been avoiding or do that task that you haven't wanted to do. This will create more coping space in your bottle.

Step Three: Work out unresolved life issues—Face the fears from which you have been running. If you need to enter into therapy to resolve and/or forgive these difficult issues, then just do it!!!

Step Four: Don't bottle in the first place—Deal with things as much as you possibly can, when they are presented to you. This will keep you from unnecessarily stuffing your bottle full of things you will have to deal with eventually.

Simplifying our lives is the best way to deal with stress. Remember to look to yourself, not to others, to accomplish this difficult and rewarding task. Think of stress reduction as a process that needs to be done on a regular basis, just like the household laundry. Hopefully, you don't waste a lot of time feeling frustrated because there is always something in your bottle that needs attention -- just as there is always more laundry to do.

Maintain a constant eye on what is in your bottle to determine what can be "cleaned out." This will keep stress to a minimum. Reducing your stress is a very important step in taking care of yourself. Taking care of yourself is a part of honoring yourself.

CHAPTER SIX

PAST, PRESENT, AND FUTURE

"Yesterday is a cancelled check.
Tomorrow is a promissory note.
Today is cash in hand; spend it wisely."
-- Anonymous

Most of us know people who are stuck in the past. They seem to talk about almost nothing else. This fixation with the past appears to be so blatant to everyone except the people who are stuck. Those who have never been in this difficult, emotional place may not be very sympathetic. They may say, "Why can't they get over it? They need to simply put it behind them and move on." The ones who have not been stuck feel certain that they would never find themselves in such a weak position. "Just get over it" may sound like logical advice, but it is not always easy to do when we are on the inside of the trauma looking out.

Over the years I have developed a very graphic metaphor for those times when we are "stuck." When we are struggling to cope with our life or working through a problem, it is useful to hold this picture in our mind. I call it, *THE PIT*.

THE PIT

I see myself walking along a path and coming upon an amazing pit. An overpowering stench fills my nostrils and my eyes sting in reaction to the fumes. The pit is long and wide and by my observations at least five feet deep. The telltale sign of the pit's depth is the person who appears to be doing a handstand in the muck, legs waving frantically, sticking straight up into the air.

I find it interesting that we stay in that position when we only need to stand upright and wade through the garbage to the edge and climb out. It seems so obvious to me from my safe, yet odorous place on the side. As I sit down to contemplate the situation, I recognize strong feelings of wanting to rescue this poor, "blind one" from this horrible torment. I imagine carefully sliding into the muck and wading out to convince the person to allow me to help and lead them to the side. This altruistic rescue appears honorable at first, but I quickly realize that I too could lose my footing and become stuck. Then we would be two unfortunate souls in the pit instead of one gallant rescuer and a soul in need of rescue. I also have an awareness that the same power the person used to get into this predicament could be used to climb out.

I begin to work on communicating my observations to the "lost one." This isn't easy. When all that the lost one can see, hear, taste, and feel is muck, the mumblings of another seem distant and unimportant. I persist in my belief that the truth is obvious if one will just pay attention long enough to perceive it. It takes just the right amount of time for my words to be heard.

At first my words are not understood, then they are

disbelieved. How could I understand when I am not the one who is currently "knee deep -- head first" in the muck? These emotions are followed with a reluctant acceptance but a strong fear of letting go of the current situation. It sounds something like, "This situation really stinks, but if I let go and try something different, it could be worse."

Eventually, with gentle persistence, the "trapped one" begins to believe that there might be a way to turn over and get a clear head. I realize that the speed at which this is accomplished will reveal a lot about this person. The turn over could be slow and cautious with many attempts and failures. The effort could appear to embrace the concept of change but might sufficiently sabotage the process so that no real progress is obtained. The pace also could be rapid and confident and display an inner ability to hear and process new information and act on it with determined purpose. It could also be a multitude of other responses. We each deal with, or avoid change, in our own way.

Once the "mucked one" is standing erect in the fresh air and light, it becomes more obvious that the edge of the pit is not too far away. Now the exhausted, yet "determined one" begins sludging to the side of the pit. After several slips and recoveries, faith begins to renew in the personal ability to deal with difficult circumstances.

Getting to the side can only be accomplished by the one in the pit. The best assistance I can give is encouragement to turn over, techniques to use, and guidance. I can offer coping strategies to keep striving for the edge and a hand up when the side is reached. Also, extremely important is assistance in achieving clarity in the entire process so that the valuable lessons may be learned.

Reaching the side of the pit, the "lighthearted one"

trembles noticeably, laughs out loud, and feels powerful at having overcome the muck. After some major cleanup work, the "wiser one" and I move down the path together for awhile. Later we go our separate ways to discover what challenges lie further along our paths.

DEALING WITH TRAUMA

Why do we step into such awful pits in the first place? You would think that something that large and foul would loom before us as bright and obvious as a casino in Las Vegas. Is it possible that the pit appears to be a hiding place? We seem to enter willingly, perhaps as a way to create safety from something that has frightened us or even from an uncertain future?

Some people see the pit and do whatever is necessary to avoid the unpleasantness of being stuck in the muck. Others fall in, never having seen the ghastly hole in front of them. There are those who have no clue what happened until, hopefully, when they finally get out of the pit, they see the process more clearly and learn from it.

Each of us perceives trauma from a different perspective. Something that causes a deep wound in one person may barely faze another.

In August of 1992 a fire began near Round Mountain, California. This catastrophic inferno, quickly labeled "The Fountain Fire," burned 64,000 acres and over 600 structures from Round Mountain to Burney. A woman's house along with all her worldly possessions burned to the ground. She was under-

*standably devastated. She talked about how diffi-
cult those first few days were and how a miraculous
awareness began to creep into her consciousness.
Slowly, but surely, a sense of freedom came over her.
She was no longer tied to "things" and was free to
create a simpler, less burdensome existence. She rev-
eled in this discovery. Her attempts to share her relief with other Fountain Fire victims were met with
awe, skepticism, and irritation. Some could not com-
prehend what appeared to be an insensitivity to such
devastating losses. This woman's trauma became her
triumph.*

*What impressed me so much about this woman
was that she described this wondrous response as
uncharacteristic of her usual reactions to trauma.
For some reason, somehow, she bypassed the pit and
found herself on the other side in a much more en-
lightened state of mind. Her ability to allow this to
unfold without judging it or fighting against it was
wonderful.*

I know that other Fountain Fire survivors, as well as
people from other catastrophic disasters, eventually moved
into a place of acceptance, to the other side of the pit, and
they were able to learn many valuable lessons from their
difficult experience. I am equally as certain that some people
remain forever entrenched in the problem, in the pit, and
they are unable to distinguish the muck from anything else
in their lives. Their focus is almost always on the past because the future holds too many unknowns. It doesn't matter how long someone has wallowed in the pit. It is never
too late to do what it takes to get out.

Loretta, one of many similar clients I have worked with over the years, made a firm decision 18 years ago that she would never be in a relationship with a man again. Her husband had hurt her terribly and left her with their 2-year-old daughter to raise on her own. She immersed herself in work and caring for her child and abandoned any thoughts of a life for herself.

Approaching 40 years old, Loretta awakened to a multitude of problems. She gained over 100 pounds throughout the years and developed diabetes as well. She clearly saw that she created her weight problem as an excellent barrier between her and the world. She had subconsciously wanted to be sure that her appearance, supported heavily by her general attitude of "unavailability," would preclude any chance of having to deal with a romantic relationship.

Her daughter, a beautiful, intelligent 20-year-old, was spoiled and irresponsible with a sense of entitlement that her mother would rescue her whenever a problem arose. Several times, over the years, they entered into therapy together to seek help for the daughter's behavior problems. Each time, some progress was made, but the core issues of the problems were not changed.

Both mother and daughter got fed up with the pain in their relationship. The daughter made several desperate attempts to separate herself from the overly symbiotic relationship with Loretta, but each hesitant, misguided struggle for independence ended with her mom coming to the rescue. Both individuals, dependent on the dance they had done for years, *seemed to breathe a collective sigh of relief as their pattern repeated, and they found themselves in a place they knew and found comfortable.*

When the daughter made a tremendous effort to separate, leaving with her druggie friends, Loretta attempted suicide. She entered therapy again, but this time was ready to look at herself and her life, or lack thereof. She began to set boundaries and limits and own her part of the family dysfunction.

As mom got stronger and began to move out of the familiar patterns, the daughter upped the ante in an attempt to maintain the dependent dance. She accomplished this by becoming pregnant and asked to come home to have the baby. Loretta agreed to her returning home, but with concerns about repeating old patterns she set many new boundaries and limits. The daughter entered a drug rehabilitation program and agreed to work on the problems again with more ownership and awareness than before. Loretta told her that they each had to learn to "own their own stuff" and create a healthy household.

If we look at Loretta's case within the metaphor of "the pit," we can see just when and how she decided to jump in. When her husband hurt and abandoned her, she dove into the pit because it appeared to be the safest thing to do. In fact she made herself quite at home in the muck and worked hard at digging the pit even deeper. The pit became the only thing she knew and a place of safety. It was obviously painful, but the fleeting thoughts of creating a different, possibly healthier life were terrifying.

In order to climb out of the pit, Loretta had to understand why she sought refuge in the pit in the first place. Then she needed awareness regarding the actions she took to stay upside down so she didn't have to deal with any other insights that might have been frightening. Once she turned over and saw exactly where she was, she had to develop the strength and skills to wade through the muck to reach the side.

Loretta clearly blamed her former husband for hurting and abandoning her. She felt that he "threw her into the pit." Though he may or may not have been the jerk she said he was, her response to his hurtful behavior was to avoid her feelings, hide from the world, and keep her child as safe, and as close to her, as possible. All these years she felt justified, even smug, about her original decision to avoid relationships. She now sees that she never questioned her response or realized that there were other options available.

Loretta's case history ended with her in the process of wading to the side of the pit. She currently has a clear understanding of this mucky pit and a strong determination to create a healthier, happier life. As of this writing, she is still working hard on this effort. She hopes that her daughter will begin to see her own pit but realizes that she cannot do it for her. Loretta can only share her experiences and insights and hope they help to guide her daughter in her own quest for freedom.

Hopefully both women will free themselves from their respective pits and move forward so that the baby does not grow up creating a pit of its own. Loretta does not want the unhealthy pattern repeated one more time.

Getting out of the pit is not the hardest part of the work. Getting your head out of the muck so that you can be clear enough to "see the light" is the scariest part. It takes an ability to "own your stuff." You must be willing to stop blaming others for your choice to dive into the pit in the first place.

Most of us dive into the pit many times during our lives. Think of it as retreating to "the safe zone" when you take a risk that has gone sour. Diving into the pit is not the biggest problem. The problem, the dysfunction, comes with staying or hiding in the pit. We all feel justified jumping into the pit when our feelings are hurt or we are angry and frightened. You can develop an ability to avoid going in by dealing with issues immediately. If you do find yourself "knee deep," hopefully you are feet first so your head stays somewhat clear. Then you must "own your stuff" and work your way out of the pit. This is an aspect of life that we simply must accept. No one is immune or beyond having to deal with problems. Those times when you find yourself in the pit, try your best not to "wallow" for very long.

Staying on a perfectly healthy path every second of our lives is unrealistic. Doing the best you can to use the skills you have is the challenge. The ability to see the pit in front of you, before you fall in, is a great skill in itself. This ability may not come to you until you become better at recognizing when you are already in the pit and begin using healthy coping skills to get out. It all takes time and experience.

Susan came to me to deal with the severe trauma of a brutal rape. She had her first session only a couple of days away from the first anniversary of the rape. When the trauma occurred, Susan scrambled to bury the terror, panic, and totally out-of-control feelings that were running amuck in her head. She told herself that she "should" be able to forget about it and go on with her life. As a busy, young professional she felt that she didn't have time to indulge herself with these weak feelings and would get over the "incident" much better if she pretended it never happened. The intensity of her feelings frightened her tremendously.

Susan told me about the trauma. During the attack the man taunted her with the fact that he had observed her behaviors for months, stalked her, and peered through her windows at night. He had broken into her car several times to steal insignificant personal items and had always left valuables behind in plain sight. He culminated this sick behavior by cutting the screen on her open window, slipping into her house, holding her hostage, and raping her for over six hours. After binding and gagging her, he finally left. After hours of struggling she was able to free herself enough to call for help.

When Susan entered therapy, she was in a state of crumbling denial. Her attempts to convince herself that this offense had no effect on her were not working anymore. Her bravado was overcome by fear. The nightmares, flashbacks, and uncontrollable emotions wreaked havoc on her life. She took a leave of absence from her job because she feared any lifestyle pattern that could target her again for someone else's, or even this same rapist's, psychotic fantasies. Susan withdrew from friends and family into a cocoon. She was desperately trying to feel safe. I could see that she was totally lost in "the pit" and willingly going down deeper and deeper in a vain attempt to find safety and invisibility.

Even though I had a clearer view from the outside of Susan's pit, I did not want to tell her to climb out. I assumed that the pit was serving a purpose and that I could help her explore what it was. She had created her pit in a desperate search for security and would need it until we could find other, healthier methods of feeling safe.

We started looking at the pit by examining all her symptoms. Manifestations of her fear included detailed nightmares, flashbacks (reliving the trauma) that were indistinguishable from reality, heightened anxiety, isolation, and severe depression. A bright and sensitive woman, Susan was quickly able to understand the concepts of love and fear. She began to see these behaviors as "fear" and her creation of them as her attempt to feel safe. She was not sure she wanted to leave the pit of her fears because to do so felt like letting go of the past and facing her uncertain future. She also felt that letting go would somehow minimize what she went through. Besides, she felt that she had confirmation that the world outside the pit was a very dangerous place.

Susan feared that if she stopped focusing on the rape, she would relax and again be vulnerable to attack. Her fears kept her in a fighting stance, ready for any psycho that was foolish enough to take her on. In other words, the constant stench, taste, and feel of the muck all around her served to keep her hypervigilant, always aware, of possible danger. To ask her to consider leaving the pit at this point would go against every natural instinct Susan possessed. Teaching her to doubt her instincts was not a goal of *our therapy.*

Susan left this first experience with therapy after several sessions. She understood where she was emotionally and clearly made a choice that she was not ready to do anymore work at that time. Having accomplished a few insights that lightened her torment to some degree, she decided to return to work and see how things progressed. It was difficult for her to work and make the long drive to my office once a week. She refused to see a therapist closer to home.

Things went better for Susan for about a year. She consciously tried to notice when she was functioning from a place of love or a place of fear and found this awareness alone helped her to relax many times.

Close to the second anniversary of the rape, Susan overheard a neighbor talking in the grocery store about a woman who was almost raped right there in the neighborhood. The rapist's behaviors sounded almost identical to her own trauma two years earlier, except this woman was able to fight him off and escape. Susan went into a complete meltdown. She went home and began to cry and couldn't stop. She crawled into bed and refused to leave. After three days of this Susan reached out to her mother, who lived across the country. Her mother called me and told me what was happening. I called Susan, and she reluctantly agreed to come to my office.

Now Susan was ready to do some more work to uncover her fears and deal further with this trauma. She didn't really have a choice anymore. Drowning in the pit was not an option.

CHALLENGES AND LESSONS

A newer method of viewing misfortune has begun to enter our consciousness. Instead of viewing a cold as just an unfortunate encounter with a germ or virus, complex factors such as immune system functioning as well as attitude and state of mind are being seen as relevant. It is common these days to hear someone quip "Why did you need to get this cold?"

Interesting, too, how more and more people are actually looking at the psychological aspects of illness, accidents, and trauma. It would not be totally unusual to hear a response to the above question be, "I have been saying for awhile that I needed a break. I guess I created one for myself by getting this cold and staying home." You can actually begin to break patterns of illness, such as that cold you get every winter, by recognizing these implications and learning to supply your needs in a healthier manner.

This concept insinuates that there is something we strive to gain by agreeing to enter the pit, whether it be through trauma, illness, or anything else. It shatters the illusion that we are victims of circumstance who unwittingly are thrown into the pit against our will. If so, then there must be some agreement, either conscious or subconscious, that we will participate in the trauma. Could this agreement possibly occur on a soul level? Perhaps before we entered this earthly plane, we contracted with Divine sources, or even ourselves, to provide an opportunity for awareness and challenges as well as lessons to be learned.

I would never be so insensitive to suggest to trauma survivors that they called this pain and suffering upon themselves. It does not mean that a rape victim, for example, caused the crime to occur or "asked for it." She did not consciously, or subconsciously, think, "I'll go out and get raped today so I can learn some valuable lessons. Maybe I'll purposely walk by that abandoned building and see if I can make it happen." What I am referring to is a Divine agreement that there are certain lessons we each need to learn. These lessons will be presented to us in many different ways, some small and hardly noticeable and some with varying degrees of trauma. It all depends on what it takes for us "to get it."

This is a spiritual concept that is difficult to consider until a victim becomes a survivor. I have been privileged to assist in this transformation many, many times and never cease to be awed when a trauma survivor begins to find the lessons and insights gleaned from the ordeal. This is what I mean by recognizing you are in the pit. You work as hard as it takes and for as long as it takes to get out of the pit. You allow yourself to learn the valuable lessons that are there for the taking.

When a close friend of mine was in a pit of her own and was working hard to get out, she felt pressured by some of her friends and family to "hurry up and get over it." One of her friends told her, "You've been dealing with this long enough, it's time to stop thinking about it and let it go." What her friend was trying to say was, "I hate to see you hurting like this, and I just want you to feel better." It felt to the person going through the pit as though her friend was telling her, "It hurts me too much to see you in such pain. I want you to stop talking about it so that I can feel better." She saw that it was too difficult for her friend to try to be in this supportive position, so she simply stopped talking to her about it. Her friend's admonishment to "hurry up and get over it" did nothing but silence the person in pain and only gave the illusion of progress.

My friend was not willing to give up the process she knew she had to go through. She knew she could not shove her emotions out of sight even though it would make those who cared about her the most feel better. She did become even more selective than she already was about deciding with whom she would or could share her deepest feelings. The others in her life were kept at less intimate trusting levels.

I know from my own experiences and through working with others in pain that we each take our own time to heal. If we stop the healing process prematurely, as Susan did with her rape trauma, by shoving it all under (the defense mechanisms of denial and repression), it will only come up to haunt us at some later date. We also give up the opportunity to glean whatever lessons are available from new insights we could have formed as we worked our way out of the pit.

Of course most of us would rather learn our lessons in some nice, safe manner such as a workshop or from a great book rather than by going through the pit. It would be great if this were always possible, but sometimes the lessons learned in the "soft way" do not always have the depth of experience and perception that the hard earned ones seem to have. I truly believe our best lessons are learned through adversity.

A woman I knew told me that she and her husband had made a pact with each other that they would never be unfaithful to one another. They had watched some dear friends go through this tremendous heartache and felt that they could learn a very difficult lesson through their friends' experiences. Several years later this woman put her promise aside, along with her morals and values, and had an affair with a married man. She was then a part of the creation of tremendous pain for a lot of people. I guess she needed to create this particular pit for herself to learn these difficult lessons. The lesson learned by observing her friends simply did not have sufficient impact to keep her from making the same mistakes.

It is often easy for people to **"should"** all over others. "You should have known better." "You should be dating by now, it's been two months already since you two broke up." "You've grieved long enough, you **should** get on with your life." "You **should** take my advice, then you'd be able to let it go." "It's been three days (or weeks, or months or years) now since this happened. I don't want to hear about it anymore. You **should** be over it by now." (It just fits to emphasize such a stinky word, as "should," don't you think?)

Sometimes I see people in therapy who succumbed to the **"should"** pressure. When we touch on the old hurt they shoved under, it takes them awhile to believe it is okay to process these feelings now. Once they do so, the feelings pour out of them like the hurt occurred just yesterday. This is a clear sign that they never worked their way completely out of the pit in a healthy manner.

The good news is it still works to go through the process now. The sad part is seeing all the damage the unprocessed feelings and unhealthy resolutions have caused in their lives. Loretta saw this phenomenon with her repressed feelings about the breakup of her marriage and the effect it had on how she raised her daughter. The lesson she learned was **"when you find yourself in the pit, don't** fight it, work it through until you truly get to the edge and crawl out."

If we do learn our best lessons through adversity, why don't we just recognize this and start to get the same value from our good experiences in life? It happens, of course, but not until we realize that it is possible to learn as much, if not more, from a state of Love. Until that time we tend to let the negative, fearful experiences capture our attention. Which is more clearly heard -- a whisper of love in the darkness or a blinding explosion that shatters our perceptions of our world? What each has to say is not always of equal value.

Much like those who wallow "in the pit" of the past, some people are always waiting for the future to arrive to begin their lives. "I will buy a bathing suit and go swimming when I lose weight." "When my house is paid off, I'll slow down a little and stop killing myself at work." "When the kids are grown and gone, we'll have time for each other."

There is a difference in fearing the future and preparing for the future. It is a fine line at times, too. Fearing the future has a paranoid quality loaded with self-doubt and insecurity in the safety of our world. Preparing for the future in a healthy manner strives for a balance between storing away for tomorrow and enjoying the fruits of our labors in the here and now.

It is wise to be aware of what the future may bring so that you can be prepared to take care of yourself. There is a wonderful fable about the ant and the grasshopper. All of the ants in the colony work hard storing food for the winter and creating a cozy nest while the grasshopper laughs at them and encourages them to come and play. "You can always do that later," he sings. When winter arrives, the ants are singing and dancing and enjoying their efforts, while the grasshopper is starving and freezing in the snow. Of course, in the end the ants invite him in and save his life with their generosity. This is a nice fairy tale ending, but it would not be fair or wise of the grasshopper to assume he will always be taken care of by others if he does nothing to contribute to his own care.

If you constantly live for the future, always viewing yourself there, you will wait to live your life until some magic happens. You will feel cheated if the future never arrives. The future is here in our grasp. It is the here and now. If your goal has been to never feel the intensity of the emotions that come with life, you will always be waiting to begin living.

Living in the here and now provides a variety of challenges that we must work with and adjust to on a constant basis. We tend to focus on the past and either long for or fear the future. The real work is here. It is now. How we deal with our current life situations can heal our past and enliven our future.

We've already discussed the people who get stuck in the past or the future, but is it fair to think we are only healthy if we can master the tremendously difficult techniques of always residing in the here and now? The healthiness rests in the degree of our awareness. If we can notice where we are at any given moment, we have a chance to decide if we are living in a healthy way. Much like being able to notice if you are in a place of love or fear, awareness of being stuck in the past or the future lets you reach out for help or enjoy where you are.

Fear can only exist in our focus on the past or our fear of the future. Fear in the here and now is not as common. Even in the middle of a trauma, much of the fear we feel is a fleeting reminder of something similar in the past or a fear of how this will affect the future. "I was so frightened. I thought he was going to kill me." This is a statement denoting fear of the future. "I started to shake with fear when I realized he was acting just like my ex-husband did when he was angry." This could be a fear of the past.

When trauma is experienced in the here and now, you hear statements such as: "While it was happening I just responded." "My adrenaline was pumping, and I did what I had to do." "I didn't even have time to think about it, I just reacted." "I wasn't frightened until I had a moment to think about how this could all turn out." "It wasn't until it was all over that I started crying and shaking just thinking about what could have happened." I am most certainly not judging how anyone handles trauma. We all do the best we can with what skills we have to work with. Surviving is the first order at hand, and we can look at something else as soon as it is safe.

When we experience the love that is available, it will hold our attention in the here and now. It is exhilarating! Our stress is reduced and a feeling of heightened awareness takes over. Some call this being "mindful" -- our minds full of the moment. This can occur from difficulties and from positive things in our lives.

For example, I find myself totally in the here and now when I'm clogging. Clogging is a true American folk dance that is a high-energy, fast-moving, foot-stomping type of dance that captures your heart. My husband and I have clogged for over 20 years and have taught others for about 16 years. You can't do the intricate steps and movements of clogging very well without being fully present. You can try, but you're bound to mess up if your head wanders too far for too long. This makes clogging a great stress release. The physical exercise along with focused attention feels great. You can't think about work or problems or much else while engaged in this or similar types of activities.

Music also gives us the opportunity to be in the here and now. When I play the piano, I can get lost in the music for a couple of hours. This only seems to work if someone isn't yelling "MOMMMM..." every few minutes or the phone isn't ringing off the hook. Entering that place where attention is completely focused makes nothing else matter at the moment. When all sense of time is lost, a transcendence to a quieter, more peaceful place occurs. Alerting to the surroundings brings a shock -- no, a thrill -- to find that the passage of time has been irrelevant.

Sometimes this phenomenon of totally immersing yourself into something can cause a problem. One time I sat down at the piano to play for 20 minutes until it was time to pick up my youngest daughter from school. I was startled by the phone ringing. It was the school telling me that Ashley had been waiting over an hour for someone to pick her up. Now I use a timer.

Many people talk about this same awesome experience with work, reading, hobbies, and much, much more. Riding on a roller coaster, staring at the stars, enjoying a conversation, listening to a song, and anything else that is happening in the moment can have the effect of capturing you in the here and now. Think about the things that do it for you. Aren't these the times that you've said "what a wonderful day this has been" or "I really enjoyed our time together" and truly meant it?

Let's assume that the ants in the fable were very wise

and knew how to create a balance between preparing for the future and enjoying their immediate existence. They would be able to live in relative peace and harmony and only deal with the unexpected that life deals out. During times of hardship, hopefully they would call on their experiences to help them deal with it effectively. They would continue to strengthen their wisdom by learning from each new challenge and still find time to laugh and love today. Now, if we can only learn to simplify our lives enough to create space for the heightened awareness of the here and now, we'll be on our way to so much more.

Living life as a journey and not a destination focuses us on where we are at the moment. Imagine driving along a beautiful coast highway thinking only of what needs to be done when you arrive at your journey's end. Missing the obvious beauty is a shame — a lost opportunity. Some people live an entire lifetime without ever enjoying the journey. The journey is the here and now and one of the greatest gifts ever given. Cherish it. Don't wait. Start now.

The Road Not Taken

Two roads diverged in a yellow wood,
And sorry I could not travel both
And be one traveler, long I stood
And looked down one as far as I could
To where it bent in the undergrowth;

Then took the other, as just as fair,
And having perhaps the better claim,
Because it was grassy and wanted wear;
Though as for that, the passing there
Had worn them really about the same,

And both that morning equally lay
In leaves no step had trodden black.
Oh, I kept the first for another day!
Yet knowing how way leads on to way,
I doubted if I should ever come back.

I shall be telling this with a sigh
Somewhere ages and ages hence:
Two roads diverged in a wood, and I --
I took the one less traveled by,
And that has made all the difference.

-- Robert Frost

LIFE
IS A JOURNEY...

NOT
A DESTINATION!!

CHAPTER SEVEN

HONORING YOURSELF

*"Build your character
thoughtfully and
painstakingly."*
-- Mark Twain

"Honor" is an interesting word that has slipped significantly from our vocabulary since it was a guidepost for behavior many years ago. The Knights of the Round Table spoke of gallantry and honor. They make us conjure up images of damsels in distress and brave, handsome men putting fears of personal safety aside to rescue their fair maidens. Honor meant that your word was your bond, and you guarded your oath of loyalty with your life.

What characteristics do we apply to this word today? Do we teach it to our children through example and instruction? If to honor someone means to hold that person in special esteem or respect, do we actually give that gift to others? Do we give that gift to ourselves?

One of the most important concepts that is a basis of a life of honor is called *PERSONAL RESPONSIBILITY*. The act of being accountable for one's actions is at the very heart of this premise. This means that the use of the defense mechanisms of denial, blaming, justifying, and minimizing are not an option. Relying on these avenues simply deludes your personal responsibility until it is so weak that it cannot be felt or acknowledged. I refer to the act of accepting personal responsibility as *"OWNING IT."*

I recently read several newspaper articles about a local college softball coach whose team had to forfeit over 20 wins for the season due to an enrollment error. One of the players, inadvertently, was not put on the class registry which made her two units short of the 12 units required to be a qualified player on the team. Clerical errors like this seem to be common these days in our busy, stressful lives. It was not the error that caught my attention, it was the coach's statement. The coach, Sonny Stupek, of Shasta College, stated, "This oversight was completely my fault and I accept full responsibility for my error." There were no excuses, justifications, or blaming statements made in an attempt for Coach Stupek to minimize his responsibility.

The integrity and honor displayed by Coach Stupek modeled more for the students at Shasta College and for everyone that read the newspaper articles than could be taught in a classroom or learned from a book. My guess is that this was an embarrassing and painful admission on this man's part, but the sense I received from the newspaper article was that he held his head high and took responsibility with honor. I was impressed with Coach Stupek's ability to "own it."

Imagine what our children would be like if from an early age we modeled owning our behavior and taught them not only how to do this themselves but also the values and benefits of behaving in this manner. Imagine this...

Your 16-year-old son strolls through the door two hours past his curfew. You're sitting in your favorite chair with that look on your face. The one that says "where-have-you-been-I've-been-worried-sick-you-better-have-a-good- excuse-or-you-are-in-really-big-trouble." You bite your tongue and state calmly and simply, with a subtle yet undeniable edge to your voice, "Well?"

Your son looks you straight in the eye with his head held high and replies, "I am two hours and five minutes late. I apologize for keeping you up and worrying you. That was inconsiderate of me."

Of course your jaw does not hit the floor with a noticeable thud because you know that you have raised this child to have honor and integrity and "own his behavior." You are not surprised at his gallant display. You are pleased that he is appropriately showing integration of this difficult concept that you have consistently and painstakingly taught and modeled for him throughout his youth.

Your look, naturally, stays firm, yet there shines a touch of pride that sparkles in your eye that your son subconsciously notices. "You will not drive the car for one week, and you are grounded to the house next weekend. In the future, if you are going to be late, I expect, and would appreciate, a telephone call with a sufficient amount of time for you to still get home within your curfew, should I deny a request for a late arrival. If there is a problem in arriving home on time, we will evaluate each situation as it comes up. I may decide to come and get you."

"I accept my punishment for my misbehavior. Thank you for your fairness. In the future, I will be more careful." He walks over and gives you a kiss

good night, which gives you the opportunity to sniff for foreign substances and get a close look at his eyes. This you do, discreetly, but you both know what is happening.

As he turns to head for his bedroom, you say with love in your voice, "Son, I'm proud of the integrity you have just displayed. I not only love you but I respect you tremendously." He acknowledges your gift with a smile.

Whoa...wouldn't that be great?! "In your dreams" you say. "Kids today just don't act like that." What if we began to teach this to them? Okay, okay...without the stuffy formality. Even if he had said, "Yo, parent-type, I'm like totally behind the clock. Whoa, like two hours late. I'm sorry, I wasn't trying to dis' you. I guess, I was like, you know, being inconsiderate." It would work, wouldn't it? The important point here is that it may be obvious that we do need to teach honor to our children, but before we can even begin this task, we must embrace the concept ourselves.

If it was never taught or modeled for us in our childhood, how do we go about learning it now? Can we change lifelong patterns of subtle, if not overt, dishonesty? Can we learn to "own it" if we already feel that not too many people like us or respect us as it is? What if owning something comes with a possible consequence that would be more than we could bear? Why "own it" if it may not be discovered by anyone?

Honor is, and should be, a very personal thing. We cannot decide for someone else what and how they should own something. If we are not the one responsible for something, do we know all the facts, motives, and emotions behind the incident? Unless people take us into their confidence and ask us for our opinion or advice, we cannot assume to know.

I was counseling a couple because the woman had breast cancer that had metastasized to several vital organs. She and her husband were dealing with the anger and grief while trying to prepare their son, Josh (15), and daughter, Cassie (12), for the difficult times ahead. Both children were aware of their mother's cancer but did not yet know of the dismal prognosis.

In the third family session, the parents were expressing concern that the stress of the illness was creating changes in Cassie's behavior. Specifically, a five-dollar bill was missing from the father's dresser top. Since Cassie was seen walking out of the bedroom not long after the father had emptied his pockets, they felt certain she had taken it.

During the fight at home, Cassie denied taking the money and was extremely upset at being accused of stealing. The parents had lectured her about character, taking responsibility, and honesty. Cassie had stubbornly refused to "own it." Now in the session, Cassie crumpled into tears and said, "Okay, I took it. Is that what you want to hear? I took it and I don't care." She was crying with a look of defiance on her face.

Her parents decided that she would have to pay back the money and would be grounded for two weeks for stealing and two weeks for lying. We worked it out that Cassie could get one day off her grounding punishment for every day of "good time" that she accomplished. They told her that they were proud of her for finally owning her behavior. Cassie looked sullen.

Two months later while moving the furniture in the bedroom to accommodate a hospital bed, the father found a five-dollar bill behind his dresser. He was mortified. The family gathered around Mom's bed and both parents apologized to Cassie for doubting her integrity.

When asked why she admitted to something she didn't do, Cassie replied, "It was obvious no one was going to believe me. It wasn't worth getting everyone, especially Mom, all upset. It really made me mad that you thought I would do something like that when I never have before."

The parents wanted to try to make up for the time Cassie was unfairly grounded, but Cassie said quietly, "It's okay. I wanted to stay home with Mom anyway."

It is always best, if a person can "own it" without being coerced or shamed into it. It is the spontaneous, unrehearsed, unexpected acceptance of personal responsibility that always means the most and creates the ultimate respect for that person. It's pretty easy to own something really wonderful that happens. It takes true character to own the tough stuff.

As I was writing this chapter and searching my mind for a case history displaying a positive example of a parent/child interaction regarding teaching honor and integrity, my friend Kathryn called. She had a problem she wanted to brainstorm with me regarding her 14-year-old daughter, Julie.

Kathryn told me that they had caught Julie in a lie and were going to confront her about it that night, but she didn't want a recurrence of past confrontations where everyone was yelling and upset. At the time I told Kathryn, "What a coincidence, that's exactly what I'm writing about in the chapter that I'm working on today." In retrospect I see the gift as a miracle that was offered to me to pass on to you. It is so special when those little, wondrous miracles occur in our lives.

Back to Kathryn's dilemma...

Kathryn explained to me that Julie had gone shopping the night before with a friend and her mother. When she came home, she told Kathryn and her dad, Rob, that she had borrowed some money from her friend's mom to buy shoes to match her graduation dress. Kathryn told her that was great because they had been looking for shoes to match the dress and hadn't been successful. Julie said the shoes had been on sale for $23, and she needed to repay her friend's mom.

The next morning on the way to school Julie asked her dad for $34 to pay for the shoes. Rob said, "I thought the shoes were $23."

Julie replied, "No, they were $34."

Rob thought he must have misunderstood her the night before. He assumed he did one of those "dad things" and tuned out as soon as Julie and Kathryn started discussing shoes and dresses. He told Julie he'd take care of it.

Before leaving for work, he mentioned the $34 to Kathryn, who immediately said, "Something is wrong *here."*

Later that morning she checked the price of the shoes at the store where Julie bought them and found out they were $23. Rob called the friend's mom who took the girls shopping and arranged to drop off a check. He casually asked her how much he owed her and she said, "Julie borrowed $49 for shoes and a pair of shorts." Rob paid her.

After work Rob and Kathryn put it all together and decided they needed to confront Julie. That's when Kathryn called me. She was angry and hurt that Julie would lie. The assumptions were flying. "She probably didn't want to pay for the entire price of the shorts out of her own money. I'm surprised she didn't try for the whole $49. She knew she wouldn't get it because we already bought her summer clothes," she stated angrily. "It makes me really upset that she would plan this out. It's so devious."

Kathryn and Rob knew that Julie was a good kid -- extremely gifted in intelligence, music, and athletics. They weren't afraid that she was becoming a juvenile delinquent. The most important question Kathryn asked was, "How do you get it across to a kid that being dishonest is wrong, and it will hurt you and everyone around you?"

"That's the lesson you want to teach her," I replied. "Put into words the values you want her to learn."

"I want her to learn the things you were telling me that chapter in your book is about, honor and integrity," Kathryn reflected.

"You have such a great opportunity here," I said

getting excited. I very seldom get an opportunity to help someone before they handle a situation. Clients often come into the office after the crisis, and we talk about ways to make it go better next time. Kathryn is an extremely developed person spiritually and is a very intelligent woman. She understood immediately when I said, "You need to approach Julie from a place of love, not fear. If we assume that your anger and hurt are coming from a place of fear, tell me what you are afraid of."

"I'm afraid she won't learn this lesson about honor and integrity. That she's telling us a lie because she doesn't respect us or thinks we're stupid and won't find out. I'm afraid if she ends up being a dishonest person, her life won't go in the direction that will lead her to happiness," Kathryn replied thoughtfully. She was beginning to get excited. "I can't believe this. I don't normally think about things so negatively. Geez, this mother thing we do sure clouds our thinking, doesn't it?"

I laughed, having done this cloudy thing with my two girls many times. "Sometimes we just can't see the forest for the trees. We all need a little help stepping back and putting into practice what we already know."

"I see that I need to approach this with love. I can do that," Kathryn said. "I'm not clear on how exactly we teach her the lesson. She needs to be punished for this, and she's probably going to go ballistic when she finds out that she'll miss the dance this Friday. I can see a huge battle coming even if we approach her from a place of love."

"When you walk into the room, go in calmly and quietly. Know that you aren't there to win a power struggle but to teach her a lesson about honor and integrity. Share all of this with Rob so that you go together as a united front. If Julie begins to respond with fear, you stay in a place of love. Her fear may sound like anger, defensiveness, blaming, or tears. If she stays in a place of love, give her lots of feedback about how that's helping the discussion go well."

"We're going to ground her for a week. If her attitude gets totally out of control, we'll add another week," Kathryn decided. "I can do this from a place of love because I really believe this is important for her."

"What are you going to do if she owns it?" I asked, thinking optimistically.

At first Kathryn made some noises like "I don't think so" and "keep dreaming." These gave over to "that would be great" and "I never thought of that."

"You and Rob have been working with all three of your kids about learning to 'own it,' so you have to be prepared that she is understanding it and will hopefully apply it to this situation," I cautioned.

"I hope she does, but she still needs to be punished for lying," Kathryn said thoughtfully. "Do we let her off completely if she owns it?"

"If she owns it, and I mean really owns it completely, I would tell her that because she showed honor and integrity by owning her mistake, her punishment is going to be very light. I'd let her know how proud I was of her and that I really respect her for owning it."

"Okay, that's good. If she owns it, we'll only ground her through the weekend," Kathryn decided.

"What if you grounded her through the weekend, but told her if she accepted her punishment with as much honor and integrity as she has shown in owning her mistake, then she can earn a reduction in her time to just before the dance on Friday night?" I offered.

"I like that. If she owns it, I really want to recognize that behavior and show her how much we respect it. I feel really good about this. I'm going to go talk to Rob so we can talk to Julie now. Thanks for the help," Kathryn said excitedly.

"That's what friends are for. You help me see the forest, I help you see the forest," I said truthfully.

The next morning, I called Kathryn and asked, "How did it go last night?"

"I am so jazzed," Kathryn replied with enthusiasm, *"Julie owned the whole thing. She was great. She told us how she planned to pay for the shorts with her own money. At the last second, while asking her dad for the check, she decided to see if she could throw in some of the extra for the shorts with the shoe money. She told us that the minute she did it, she felt badly and almost called from school that day to fix it. You know, I was assuming all the wrong things and it was fueling my fear. I had myself assuming the worst. Why do we do that to ourselves?"* Kathryn asked.

"It's that 'illusion of safety' thing I told you about. You were trying to protect yourself from more hurt,"

I reminded her.

"Oh, yes, I remember that now. Anyway, a couple of times Julie started to escalate, but she heard me when I told her that things would fair much better for her if she could stay calm and discuss this with us. Then she did it!! She calmed down and talked!!! Rob and I were so impressed and we told her so."

"I'm so thrilled for all of you," I said sharing her excitement. "It sounds like all three of you did a great job."

"Patty, it was like breaking the mold. I normally would have walked into that room angry and defensive, and it would have all fallen apart from there. I am so glad we talked about it first. It let Rob and me do it differently, and Julie followed our lead. I feel like it's going to be much easier for all of us to deal with this normal kid stuff in a better way."

"'Breaking the mold.' I really like that. Can I use that in the book?" I asked, my wheels beginning to turn fast. "In fact, Kathryn, this is just the type of example I was looking for. Would you, Rob, and Julie let me put the entire thing in the book, just like it happened?"

Kathryn talked to Rob and Julie. They thought it would be a great thing to share with other families. So...there it is.

THE THREE TYPES OF LIES

The only behavior that gets in the way of owning your behavior is dishonesty. We can dance around the truth through justifications, minimizing, blaming, excuses, and denial, but basically we are simply being dishonest, at least to ourselves.

When we lie, we must be in a place of fear. With some lies the thing we are afraid of is obvious. Some of the possibilities are fear of punishment, embarrassment, rejection, or looking foolish. If we were truly loving ourself at the moment, it would be easier to own whatever it was we felt we had to lie about.

I often hear people coaching others to lie. "Just tell your boss you were delayed by a train stopped on the tracks." If I were the boss, I would have more respect for the person who simply said, "I'm sorry I'm late, I just couldn't get my act together this morning. I'll make the time up." Of course if it really was a train, then telling the truth will usually ring clear.

Most of us are not really good at telling an outright lie, and our faces clearly show it. This could be because when we lie, we are in a place of fear and it's the fear that really shows. When people learn to lie without feeling fearful, it shows how much practice they have had and how confident they feel in their ability to hide the truth. It becomes easier each time to vary from the truth, sometimes so easy that they can convince themselves that's what really happened. Having a reputation as a smooth liar is the opposite of a reputation of honor and integrity. How embarrassing can you get?

Any act without honor and integrity in it shows a

lack of confidence in oneself and the world. Why would a person steal? Possibly there is a sense of entitlement that the world owes him due to something that has angered or hurt him. It could also be that the person does not believe that he could make it in the world relying on himself. These are feelings of fear that get in the way of honor and integrity. All of us have known people who, in spite of hardship, anger, pain, and difficulties, still live their lives in an honorable manner. The people who value their honor and integrity above all else are wise indeed. When they can follow their beliefs even when times are tough, they have the strength of character to endure whatever hand life deals.

LYING BY COMMISSION

The first and most obvious form of lying is "lying by commission." This is actually saying something that you know is false. If your child tells you that he did brush his teeth and you happen to notice how dry the toothbrush is as you're straightening the bathroom, it will cross your mind that you've been told a lie. Hopefully you won't assume but will ask him why the toothbrush is dry if he did indeed brush his teeth. Unless he can produce a spare, wet toothbrush from the drawer, you may get a little upset. This would be a lie by commission. It has been called "a bold-faced lie."

Picture the same parent in the local smorgasbord taking the family out to dinner. The cashier asks how old the boy is as they charge for children based on their age. The parent looks her right in the eye and states, "He's 10 years old." The boy starts to say, "I turned 11..." but the slight nudge to his side quickly quiets him down. For some strange reason, the same parent who was justifiably upset when the son lied about brushing his teeth feels justified in lying about the child's age because he saved $.59. The value of this parent's honor just became $.59, and the example set for the son was a lesson he obviously would not forget.

LYING BY OMISSION

Leaving out important information is called "lying by omission." If a lie of this sort happens in error, a person of honor and integrity will do what is necessary to correct the problem. I remember the time my good friend, Patti Burbach, asked me for my recipe for spaghetti because she loved it. I wrote down the recipe from memory because I made it all the time and knew it by heart. Several months later, Patti was eating my spaghetti at my house and exclaimed, "I can't believe you lied to me. You put onions in here and you didn't write that on the recipe. I thought it tasted differently when I made it."

"Oh, Patti, I'm so sorry," I apologized, "I would never do something like that on purpose. I should have looked at the recipe card when I wrote it down for you." I felt really sheepish. How do you prove something like that?

"I didn't think you'd do that. It isn't like you," Patti replied.

"Thanks." I felt good about myself and about Patti.

Let's try a different example...

Your teenager tells you she's going to the movies with a couple of girlfriends, and she'll be home by 11 o'clock. When she comes in, on time, you ask her how the evening was and she says it was great. How was the movie, you ask, and she tells you a few details and heads off to her room. The next day a friend of yours mentions seeing your daughter with a bunch of teenagers "hanging out on the cruise." Hmmmm...

When you confront your daughter about the "cruise sighting" she says defiantly, "I didn't lie to you. I left with Kristin and Lauren, we stopped to pick up Katy, and we went to the movie. I was home on time, so what's the big deal?"

"You did lie to me! You didn't mention that you were out on the cruise," you persist in an attempt to get her to "own it."

"You didn't ask me so I didn't lie," she expounds with false bravado.

For a moment you falter, thinking, "That's true, I didn't ask her." You quickly regain your tentative position of authority and state firmly, "I shouldn't have to ask you. You left out an important detail of your evening and that is called 'lying by omission.' You will gain my trust and respect if you behave with honor and integrity by being completely truthful. You are grounded from any activities for two weeks. As usual, you have the opportunity to decrease your punishment by one day for each day you are cooperative and have a good attitude."

Of course you are not foolish enough to think that she'll be awed into silence by your eloquent speech, but your logic is sound and if your consistency is there, she'll get it eventually. Hopefully, she'll get it in time for you to reap some of the harmony before she's grown up and moves out of the house.

LYING BY ASSENT

When you allow someone to believe something that you know is not true, you are "lying by assent." This doesn't mean you're supposed to stick your nose into everyone's business or correct every little thing you hear. Telling the people talking to each other in front of you at the grocery store that the movie they're discussing was not as good as they say is probably not going to be welcomed. However, in your interactions with others, it is your responsibility to be sure you are understood.

For example, your wife asks if you paid the rent and you reply, "It's been taken care of." You know full well that she will now assume that means you did indeed pay the rent. How is she to know that means you knocked on the landlord's door and told him, in no uncertain terms, that if he ever calls your place again and tells you the rent is late, he'll regret it. She might suspect otherwise only if you have one of those reputations that is the opposite of a reputation of honor and integrity.

Here's a hint: If you have developed a style that requires people to ask exactly the right question to get an honest answer from you, it is time to work on the concept of honor and integrity. Your justifications that you aren't exactly "telling a lie" have just been blown for what they really are -- lies of omission and assent, also called dishonesty.

Honor, much like loving, needs to be embraced personally before it will have the depth and texture necessary to have substance when giving it to others. To behave in an honorable manner, we each need to develop a strong character with integrity, honesty, respect, and a multitude of other positive characteristics that support this valuable concept.

Clients often tell me of troubled and abusive childhoods where honor and integrity were far from what was actually modeled. Many of these people do not live a life as adults like the one they experienced growing up. They do not abuse or molest their children or anyone else's children. They hold down responsible, reliable positions with jobs and families. I see integrity in people that would be hard pressed to identify the role model who taught them these values. Someway, somehow along the way, they grasped, to some degree, the concepts required of them to make it in today's world.

It has been said that it only takes one person in a child's life who exemplifies the characteristics of a person with honor and integrity for that child to grasp hold of and have the opportunity to follow the lead. On numerous occasions clients have told me, "I had a horrible childhood, but this one teacher...or my grandparents or this coach or my older brother or my best friend's mother... showed me how we are to treat ourselves and others." Any person who touches another human life has the opportunity to give a wondrous gift. A moment of honor goes a long way, an hour even further, and a position of consistent contact marked with honor and integrity can change a life—even a simple observation can make a difference.

Glenda, an intelligent, 30-year-old woman, sought therapy to deal with her abusive childhood. Her father was an alcoholic who, when drunk, abused her mother as well as Glenda and her brother. Glenda spoke of screaming and fighting with dishes shattering like it was a nightly occurrence. There was never any money, and they moved often to stay ahead of the bill collectors.

After quite awhile of processing and exploring Glenda's traumas and working on many therapeutic issues, we began exploring her honor and integrity. I told her, "I'm very impressed with how you have developed such a strong, healthy character with amazing honor and integrity after growing up in such a difficult environment. Do you know how you accomplished it?"

Glenda reflected for a few minutes and then spoke very softly. "Christmas was always the hardest time for me. I can only remember one Christmas tree that my father brought home, and that one was ruined the next night in one of his rages. Occasionally, my brother and I would get a nice gift but never the one we really wanted. Usually it was something my mom bought from a thrift store by scraping change together. She tried hard, I guess.

"Whenever the fighting would start," she continued, "I would grab my little brother's hand and go outside to wait it out. Sometimes we would walk up and down the blocks around the neighborhood, and I would watch the windows as we walked by. I'd show my brother the beautifully decorated trees with packages peeking out from underneath. We'd see families sitting down for dinner together and hear music playing. Kids were laughing and grown-ups were smiling. That's how my house is going to be, I'd tell my brother. That's how it's supposed to be."

Who touched your life with honor and integrity? Have you ever told this person or these people? What a wondrous opportunity to bring these values full circle by returning their gift with a similar one of your own -- the gift of appreciation. If there is no one in your life whom you can identify with these values, and you want it, begin by living a life of honor and integrity, and you will give the gift to yourself. Look for it in others and comment when you see it. It really is all around us if we open our eyes.

CHAPTER EIGHT

HONORING RELATIONSHIPS

"The purpose of a relationship is to decide what part of yourself you'd like to see 'show up,' not what part of another you can capture and hold."
-- Neale Donald Walsch

Creating a good relationship is very important to most people. Pairing and mating drives are instinctual; however, the skills to develop a successful relationship do not come as naturally. Living a life of personal honor and integrity creates a foundation on which your relationship can grow. Combine your instincts with personal and relationship skills, and a winning combination is created.

Learning new skills can feel overwhelming at first, but with patience and practice they become second nature. We can choose a multitude of examples to demonstrate this truth: learning to walk, learning a sport or game, playing a musical instrument, memorizing multiplication tables, to name a few. The greatest opportunities for learning we have been given are the challenges we face in our relationships.

We must keep in mind that there are varying levels of relationships. In Chapter Two you learned about "Trusting Levels" which explained how relationships move from the superficial level of the "Acquaintance" to the deeply personal characteristics of a "Level Five" or "Intimate Level" of interaction. One of the most significant factors differentiating the "Trusting Levels" is the amount of time you spend with that person. Directly proportional to the amount of time spent in a relationship is the degree of expectations that we hold for that interaction. Our expectations seem to rise and become more complicated the more involved we become with someone.

Expectations are attempts to meet needs for ourselves when we form a close alliance with another individual. Some people would like to think that they entered into their relationships to only give of themselves to their mate. "I seek only to love others and do not give any thoughts to my own needs or desires." On the surface this sounds very altruistic, but with a deeper look, it's a little scary. How could someone find themselves so unimportant that they do not deserve to be "given to" as well as allowed "to give." There would be no balance in a relationship such as this, and it would be doomed for serious problems.

Realistically, we all seek out relationships that complement or even challenge who we are. This includes what we are able to bring as our gifts to another and what we need and allow ourselves to receive from the other individual. This goes for acquaintances, friends, good friends, best friends, and those that we hold in the most intimate places in our hearts.

Let's look at some of the needs we have that we seek to meet in our relationships:

- A feeling of being loved
- Acceptance
- Understanding
- Security

- Safety
- Caring
- Stability
- Consistency
- Protection
- Being taken care of
- Sense of family and/or belonging
- Hopefully, a place to return all of the above to the ones we love.

If we were raised in a loving, trusting environment, these needs were probably provided for us to some degree. Seeking to either recreate this type of environment, or possibly create it for the first time in your life, is a healthy thing. Sometimes people think that they have entered into a relationship where these needs have been promised, even though this may have occurred nonverbally. Often it is the perceived "breaking of this unspoken contract" that creates the beginning of problems. We begin to feel cheated and betrayed when the other person does not, or cannot, follow through with meeting our needs.

How we behave in our relationships can be a mirror into our soul if we take the opportunity to look. A classic example is from the Grimms' Fairy Tale, "Snow White and The Seven Dwarfs." Let's take a few liberties and read between the lines of the interaction between the Queen and her magic mirror.

"Looking glass upon the wall, who's the fairest of us all?" demands the Queen, feeling certain of her answer.

The mirror, knowing the expected answer, replies,

"You are fairest of them all."

The next day the Queen goes to the mirror looking for her ego stroke of the day. "Looking glass upon the wall, who's the fairest of us all?" she asks.

After awhile the mirror decides not to compromise its own integrity anymore and tells the Queen the truth. "I can't stand this anymore," hollers the mirror. "I've been lying to you for years. I've compromised my own honor and integrity because I was fearful of what you would do to me. The truth is, oh short-sighted one, that Snow White is far more beautiful than you. Oh yeah, the babe has looks, but that's not what I'm talking about. The girl is beautiful inside and out. She cares about people, animals, and the world, which is far more than I can say about you. You live in constant fear and cannot even see it. Take a hint from Snow White who is a light of love. Think less about how you look to others, my Queen of darkness, and more about who you are inside."

If we look to our relationships to be our "ego stroke of the day," what happens if we don't get it? It may cause some pain, but it creates an opportunity to look into ourselves. Imagine the Queen saying, "You're right, oh wise and faithful mirror. I have known for some time now that I have been unhappy and need to reevaluate my life. I will heed your advice and learn how to find this light of which you speak." Then again, the Queen could get royally ticked at the mirror, feel cheated and betrayed, and lose the opportunity to look at herself.

A typical problem I hear in couple therapy is that one party is extremely needy and is constantly looking for praise, reassurance, and acknowledgment. This may have even been attractive to each person in the beginning of the relationship because each partner is getting a need met. It feels wonderful to "the needy one" because it feels as though someone finally understands and is willing to give tons of positive attention. The other partner becomes "the giving one" in the relationship, which can fit his or her need to be needed and to take care of or fix someone else.

After awhile the novelty of "the needy one" and "the giving one" relationship can wear off, and each begins to feel resentful and angry. "The giving one" probably assumed that if large quantities of praise, reassurance, and acknowledgment were given, then the partner would heal and someday begin to give back and make it all worthwhile. When this does not occur, "the giver" begins to feel betrayed, hurt, and angry. "The needy one" begins to look weak and unattractive, and "the giver" pulls away creating more fear and neediness in the other. The more fear and neediness, the more "the giver" pulls away, and more fear is created. Soon you have a relationship of fear that is falling apart, and everyone is unhappy and blaming each other.

One of the ways to heal this unhealthy type of interaction is to take the opportunity the pain is presenting and look at yourself. Why did you choose a partner such as this? What needs of yours did this relationship promise to meet? What were your expectations of your partner? Did you expect him or her to be able to meet your every need for the rest of your life with the same intensity as in the beginning of the relationship? If you are "the giver," did you expect to be able to give so much love, attention, and guidance that your partner would spontaneously heal and become the person you wished for in the beginning of the relationship?

"He constantly has to be told what a great job he's doing. It drives me nuts. I feel like making a recording with all the compliments and praises so he can play it 24 hours a day. He takes out the trash and wants me to fall all over myself acknowledging and thanking him for helping me. I've really begun to resent it. I find myself looking for ways to avoid his little ego stroking setups. It's almost less effort for me to take the trash out myself. It feels like such a set-up because if I don't say just the right thing, he pouts or gets angry. It feels so phony now because I never get a chance to see something for myself and sincerely comment on it."

Another typical example:

"She is so insecure about everything she does. Even getting dressed for work in the morning becomes a test of my love and acceptance of her. She is constantly asking me if her clothes are okay, or does she look fat in something. Boy, don't ever touch that one or you could get your lips ripped off. Lately, she's added concerns about getting older and throws that into the inquisition, too. If I don't say just the right thing, she'll start all over with a different outfit. How does she ever get dressed when I'm not there?

"She used to be so happy and responsive to me. Now she nags and bitches all the time. I can't seem to do anything right. She's constantly telling me I'm not the same guy she married, but she isn't the same either. This goes on and on until we end up in a huge fight, she starts crying and then I feel guilty."

The other side of the story...

"He was so sweet, patient, and loving in the beginning of our relationship. He noticed every little thing: a change in my hairstyle, a new outfit, or any subtle little change in my mood. If I lost a couple of pounds, he'd notice and tell me I was looking great. I was swept off my feet because I felt as though I had finally met my Prince Charming, my soul mate. I felt so understood, taken care of, and loved. I am at my best when I'm treated this way, and I fell all over myself letting him see how much I loved and needed him.

"After we'd been together awhile, his compliments began to get fewer and farther between. He didn't seem to understand me anymore and now seems to purposely misread me. I know I responded by getting irritable and testy, but he began to feel so detached and unavailable.

"We fight all the time now. Doesn't he realize that if he just behaved like he did in the beginning, I would be able to be my wonderful, loving self? Now he's only nice when I finally break down and cry."

If any of the these people looked at themselves in these relationships, they might make some surprising discoveries. They might learn what drives them to do what they do. When you spend most of your time and energy blaming someone else for your problems, the opportunity for self-reflection waits like a wonderful, insightful book on the shelf. You can't learn anything until you open it and read it.

A constant need to be validated by others is an indication that a person is living in "Fear." Remember that fear is basically "mistrust" -- primarily mistrust of self. Somehow this fearful person has learned to look outside of self to others to feel good. If a person learns to look within to validate or judge personal behaviors, then the concepts of self-reliance, consciousness, and love can be learned. Once these principles are practiced on ourselves, they become easy to give as gifts to others.

SELF-RELIANCE WITHIN A RELATIONSHIP

How does someone come to doubt their own judgment and to look to their relationships for validation of who they are? What are they afraid of if they don't get it? How do you learn to look for love within? One likely place to look for these answers is in your childhood.

"Mom, does this outfit look good on me?" my 14-year-old daughter, Tara, asked as she scrutinized herself in the mirror.

"Sure, it's cute on you," I answer brightly. I notice an odd feeling in my stomach as this interaction begins. We've been on this road before. She asks, I answer positively, she asks if I'm sure, I answer more positively, and she gets more specific ("do my legs look too white?" or "does this stick out funny?" or "do I look fat?"). It pushes my guilt buttons about passing on some of my old eating disorder garbage. I tune into the message in my gut.

"Tara, honey, what are you afraid of?" I ask in

that calm, quiet voice that is trying to sound support-ive, not judgmental.

"I just don't want to look bad. Everyone will laugh or make stupid comments. I hate getting dressed for school."

"So what are you afraid of?"

"I don't know. Geez, mom, do you have to do this right now. I just want to know if these shorts look okay," she states with that exasperated, do-you-have-to-put-your-therapist-hat-on-again, voice.

"Okay, do you want the short version?"

Tara nods her head with a slight, yet noticeable roll of her eyes that clearly states, "If I have to."

"I think you looked in the mirror and decided for yourself that this outfit was either acceptable or not. Because you don't trust your own opinion, you asked me. You're looking for me to agree with whatever your decision was that you already made inside. Then you can feel good about your ability to judge how you look. Your fear of being rejected by the kids at school is really strong, as it is for most teenagers (okay, a lot of adults, too), and this fear drives you even harder to check out your own opinions. Would you like to do this differently?"

"Okay. How?" Tara sighed.

"Look in the mirror and ask yourself if this outfit is okay." I instructed. "What is your answer?"

"It's all right. It isn't perfect, but it's okay for school," she replied hesitantly.

"Now, believe yourself. Trust in your own obser-vations and opinions. If you feel fearful, it probably has nothing to do with the clothes you're wearing."

"I can do that, but is it bad if I still get other people's opinions sometimes?" Tara asked.

"Of course not, we all need reassurance at times. It's like anything else in life, we need to have balance. If we always look outside ourselves for validation, we never learn how to give it to ourselves."

If we were raised to always look to our parents for guidance, how do we learn to find strength in ourselves when someone is not available to take care of us? The history of our society is such that little boys were usually raised to be independent and self-reliant and to learn to follow their logical, intellectual thought processes to make decisions. Little girls were traditionally raised to be caring and sensitive to the needs of others and to rely on their intuition and emotional input in relating to the world. There were always exceptions to these patterns, but long ago and hopefully to a lesser degree today, these people were considered outside the norm. Statements such as "she has the business sense of a man" or "he is emotional just like a woman" or even "Mr. Mom" reflect the stereotypes that society creates.

It has been a typical experience of a woman to be raised to look to "her man," whether that be her father or her husband, to make important, logical decisions. Many men were raised to look toward the woman in their life to take care of their emotional needs and anything that fell into that more sensitive category. Social calendars, gifts, holiday preparations, children, and elderly relatives are just a few examples of what has fallen into this "sensitive and emotional" arena.

As we gain awareness and grow as a society, we

begin to break out of these stereotypes and push the limits of old comfort zones. However, an interesting phenomenon does tend to happen. It is not unusual for a "modern-thinking" man or woman to fall back into traditional stereotypes once they enter into a marriage. This tendency is especially strong if the person's parents had a marriage that followed traditional roles. We seem to lean toward what we know, and it can take incredible amounts of self-awareness to change the unhealthy or unfair parts of these patterns.

I often find that even the clients who are very high-functioning individuals in their lives outside their relationship can be very dependent and insecure within the relationship. That old saying "we never know what goes on behind closed doors" is very true. A high-powered executive that makes multimillion-dollar decisions on a daily basis can be hesitant and fearful within a relationship. Professionals trained to deal with people can become uncommunicative, angry, and defensive when dealing with their significant other.

"We were having this huge fight because I found out I had to go into work on the weekend we planned to go away by ourselves. George was furious at me and would not even listen to my explanation. I couldn't believe what happened next. The phone rang. It was one of George's clients calling to reschedule an important meeting because of some scheduling conflict. George was a perfect, professional gentleman. He listened and told the guy it was no problem. They worked out another time, chatted comfortably for a few minutes, and hung up. George turned around and started yelling at me

again without even missing a beat."

How do we remain so reasonable and understanding with others and keep our high expectations and dependencies with our mates? It isn't as simple as understanding the "Trusting Level" a person occupies in our life. We can be as compassionate with a deep "Level Five" friend who has disappointed us as we are with an important business acquaintance. The incredible depth of our intimate, mate relationship must touch us on a core, soul level that triggers feelings and responses that other relationships do not even begin to touch.

It is no accident that our relationships offer us such a rich and fertile ground in which to grow. We are given the opportunity in our relationships to witness our own strengths and weaknesses with great intensity. How we avail ourselves of this wondrous gift is the secret to self-growth and therein a healthy relationship.

Barbara and Todd entered into marital counseling in a last attempt to reconcile. This was the second separation in their 23 years of marriage. The first separation was several years back following Todd's affair with another woman. After a six-month separation they had reunited and attempted to pick up where they left off before Todd chose to have the affair. That reunification lasted only a couple of years before they split again.

One of the first issues in their marital therapy was the unresolved issues surrounding the affair. Barbara's hurt, anger, and mistrust had deepened and festered. Her intense emotions were seen as pun-

ishment by Todd. He alternated between trying to be understanding, demanding when she was going to put this "thing" behind her so they could go on, and feeling intensely guilty and resentful. Each was pointing the finger of blame at the other saying that if he/she would just change, then we would be okay.

A significant amount of time was spent looking at the developments in their relationship, communication issues, behavior patterns, and intimacy issues that led to the affair. During this time Barbara and Todd did some individual counseling, as well, to become aware of their own personal issues.

We worked on healthy communication, coping skills, trusting, and intimacy issues so that the current relationship could continue to grow as the old issues were worked out.

One of the major breakthroughs in Barbara and Todd's therapy was the awareness that their personal, core issues affected the relationship. Todd recognized that his tendency to feel guilty about everything was his attempt to control his environment and the people in it. If he felt guilty, it must be his fault. If it was his fault, then it was his responsibility to fix whatever was wrong. Being an extremely intelligent, sensitive individual, Todd would proceed to logically rectify the situation. When his attempts to fix things didn't work, he would become resentful and angry. After trying hard many times to "fix" Barbara's hurt and anger over the affair, Todd became more and more sullen, withdrawn, and depressed. After several years of "trying hard," Todd decided it was never going to "be okay" and he moved out. Recognizing he still

loved Barbara, he agreed to work on the relationship.

Todd began to see his guilt and resentment as fear.
He realized that he was afraid of rejection by Barbara. One of his core issues was a fear of "not being
good enough." This drove him to take responsibility
for everything around him and then to become resentful and angry at the burden. Todd's awareness
began to free him from his fear. He learned to look
to himself instead of blaming Barbara for not re-
sponding correctly to his attempts to fix her.

Todd, before Barbara, began to see the difficult
concept that we must allow everyone to experience
their own fear. Each person's anger, hurt, depression, grief, insecurities, and all the other manifestations of fear that we come up with, must be experienced and worked through individually in order for
us to grow. Todd's attempt to take Barbara's fear
from her and fix it for her did not work because it
cannot work. The only way Barbara was going to
vanquish her fears was to own them as her own and
stop blaming Todd. She needed to take responsibility
for them and embrace them as a gift to herself. This
gift was her opportunity to look into her soul and see
what lay within.

The only way Todd could help her was to stop trying to help her. He had to learn how to hear her
fears without judgment, criticism, or attempts to fix
everything. He had to learn to respond with love and
understanding as a way of supporting Barbara without robbing her of the opportunity to grow. He had
to learn to stop taking her fears as personal attacks

on him which he saw as "not being good enough."
Although triggered by Todd's behaviors, Barbara's
fears belonged to Barbara and were not Todd's fears
to understand and change.

This awareness did not mean that Barbara was
"the problem" in the relationship. The partners came
together to do their dance and learn from each other.
Their individual strengths and weaknesses were serving to provide opportunity for themselves and each
other to look deeper into themselves to see their fear
and learn to love.

Barbara's opportunity for clarity was presented
when Todd called and asked for an individual appointment. This was not unusual as we had many
times varied between Todd and Barbara working
individually as well as the couple therapy. Todd had
not told Barbara he was thinking of coming alone
and waited to tell her until after his session. Barbara immediately responded with fear to Todd's having an individual appointment without telling her
beforehand. During the couple session several days
after Todd's individual session, Barbara expressed
her fear.

"If he had only told me he had something personal he wanted to work on, I wouldn't be so angry,"
Barbara said with the glaring eyes and trembling lip
that I had learned to associate with her most intense
fears. "He wouldn't even have had to tell me why he
was coming in. As long as I knew it wasn't about
me, I would have been fine."

When I asked her if she could identify her fears,
Barbara was able to use her new insights to identify

them. "I was afraid he wanted to talk about leaving me again. I guess that's fear of abandonment, my big fear. If he had just recognized my fear and had been considerate of my feelings, he would have told me he wanted an individual appointment. Then I wouldn't be feeling like this right now."

Although Barbara was recognizing her own fear, she was still blaming Todd for creating that fear within her. Also she was looking to Todd to protect her and not trigger her fears of abandonment. Barbara believed that Todd held the power to create or fix her fear. This belief made it difficult for her to utilize the opportunity being presented.

"I thought I was being considerate by not telling you I was coming in," said Todd. "I knew if I said anything, you would respond with fear, especially if you asked me why I wanted to go alone. I needed to talk about us. I've been concerned that we don't have enough in common and that it's always triggering your fear every time I do something without you, like play golf. I thought I'd come in and work it out within myself before I tried to share it with you."

In a very complicated, emotional session Barbara went round and round between recognizing her fear as her own and blaming Todd for creating this fear within her. At one particularly emotional point, Barbara stated, "There is an injustice that I'm causing myself that does not allow me to have any peacefulness."

I just about jumped out of my chair! "Say that again," I said to Barbara with excitement.

"Say what?" she said with a startled look on her

face. "What did I say?"

Not wanting to lose what was probably the most profound thing Barbara had said since therapy began, I wrote down what she had stated word for word. I handed her my note pad and asked her to read it aloud.

"There is an injustice that I'm causing myself that does not allow me to have any peacefulness." Barbara looked at me as if to say, "Yeah, so?"

"What is this injustice? What's another name for it?" I prompted.

"Well, I guess you would call it fear. This injustice comes from my fear, right?"

"Go on. Your fear of what creates an injustice to yourself?" I said softly, trying not to just blurt out the whole thing but allow her to unwrap the gift herself.

"Okay. I know that one of my core issues is fear of abandonment, so I guess I'm always trying to make sure that's not going to happen. I take things personally all the time, well, not as much as I used to, I have gotten a lot better at that. I get angry and controlling in order to push Todd away so he can't hurt me. That's me trying to feel safe, right?"

"Right, go on." I said softly.

"Being in that guarded kind of place makes me feel bad all the time. I can never relax and feel peaceful. Is that the injustice? I rob myself of feeling peaceful by thinking I need to be on guard at all times to keep Todd from hurting me," she answered herself.

"What is it that Todd is trying to share with you today. What statement was he making when he felt he couldn't talk to you about the things he came in *here alone to discuss?"*

"My fear was pushing him away -- keeping him out," Barbara said reflectively. "I guess my defensiveness was doing just what it was supposed to do, keep him out so he couldn't hurt me again."

"Did you assume your walls would know when to stay up and when it was safe to come down? Did you think Todd would be able to tell when it was safe to approach you and when he should stay back?" I asked Barbara.

"You know, I guess I did expect that. I think I do expect him to know me well enough and love me enough to know when and how to approach me. Isn't that how people are in a healthy relationship?" Barbara said a little defensively.

"Yes, but only after they have learned to own their fear and have worked toward their own healing. We'll get into that, when we get there. Go back to your injustice and your fear. How would you be with Todd if you didn't have the fear -- if you responded to him with love?"

"I would say to myself that I don't need to be afraid. I'm a good catch and I'm worth loving. If he doesn't see that, it's his loss," Barbara said with confidence.

"Good. Now try the same thoughts without the negativity and implied threats."

It took Barbara several tries, a few laughs, and a little bit of help, but she finally came up with, "I'm a good person. I am worth loving, and it's okay for me to relax and feel peaceful because I know that I'm going to be okay no matter what happens." We looked at the two statements side by side. Barbara's state-

ment regarding the injustice she was causing herself was clearly a statement of fear. Her statement that she was worth loving was a simple declaration of love.

"Who is it that you are loving or fearing?" I asked Barbara and Todd together.

"Each other," replied Todd.

"Yes, that is part of it, but who are you loving or fearing first before you can even begin to love or fear another?"

"It is us!! I mean it's me, isn't it? I have to love myself in order to believe in myself to know that I'm going to be okay! If I do that, it doesn't really matter what someone else does because I'll always be able to fall back on myself," Barbara said excitedly. "I think I get it. This is scary, though. What if I can't do it? What if I don't always love myself? I don't think I've ever really loved myself!"

Now we were on the right path in the therapy. It is not reaching a destination called "Love" that is important. It is the journey of learning how to love yourself and therefore being able to love others that we must strive for. First we must learn that the road to "Love" exists and following it is important. Then we must recognize when we are off the path and take the necessary steps to return. It is knowing when you've taken a side trip into "Fear" and using your skills to come back to "Love" that is the key to walking this path. We don't have to be perfect at it. We can fall into pits, stumble over obstacles, and even lose our way. Returning and continuing on the path of "Love" is what it's all about.

It is my personal belief that "Love" is the purpose for our earthly existence. Learning to love, loving ourselves, loving others, receiving love, giving love, teaching love is the essence of living. It is our fear of not having or being loved that seems to drive so much of the negativity in ourselves, our relationships, and the world. Such a complicated, yet simple idea -- the magnitude of it can change a person, a relationship, and even the world.

CHAPTER NINE

LOVING YOURSELF

"O God, help me to believe
the truth about myself,
no matter how beautiful it is!"
-- Macrina Wiederkehr

The words were loud and clear inside my head, "I love you." It startled me because I realized I was talking to myself. I don't remember where I was or what I was doing, except that it was nothing of any importance. I wasn't in the middle of some self-esteem exercise, meditating, or consciously thinking about myself at all. "I love you." There it was again, only this time I said it on purpose.

I sat down abruptly, feeling as though the wind was knocked out of me. The sensations were beyond conscious thought, they were all encompassing. I started to cry, and the tears seemed to pour from the depths of my soul. The pain seemed to come from every cell in my body. The crying seemed to last an eternity. I don't know how long I sat there like that. I don't even remember if anyone was home with me at the time. It was lucky that no one walked into the room because there would not have been any words to express what was happening to me.

The deep, cleansing, love-filled sensation that enveloped my entire being is a visceral memory that will always be a part of me. At that point in time I felt the perfect Love that makes up all that everything is. I knew the love that I felt for myself. For the first time in my life, I knew what it truly felt like to love myself. It awed and shocked me all at the same time.

I haven't shared that memory with very many people. I have never really felt moved to talk about it, until I started writing this chapter. It isn't that I would have been ashamed or embarrassed to tell someone about it; it's just that the experience defies words. It would be much like trying to explain a breathtaking sunset. Mere words could not come close.

I'll confess one more thing I occasionally do since the experience of knowing the love I felt for myself. Sometimes when I call my voice mail to check my messages, I'll leave a message that I'll hear the next time I call in. I simply say, "I love you, Patty." I have never told anyone about this. My husband, Richard, may know, because he heard me once. When I noticed he was listening, I got embarrassed and I laughed it off as a joke.

Understanding the importance of self-esteem is basic information we all need. It is an interesting process to try to understand what self-esteem is and how it develops. However, the critical idea to get across is beyond the concept of "self-esteem." It is the concept of loving ourselves.

Since my awareness of truly loving myself, I have known the difference between just having self-esteem and truly feeling deep, unconditional love for oneself. I've always felt like a capable, confident person with good self-esteem but have not always loved myself. In fact, until my experience I did not give it more thought than to quote clichés such as "we have to love ourselves before we can love someone else." If someone had asked me if I loved myself, I probably would have answered that I felt I had good self-esteem, so, yes, I would have said I love myself. I felt that self-esteem and loving oneself were one and the same. When I would hear someone use that old cliché, I would nod my head knowingly, but I didn't realize that I was so unclear regarding how to specifically achieve this goal. In talking to other people I discovered they were just as confused about what self-esteem really is and how it relates to self-love.

Once I began to see the two concepts, self-esteem and self-love, as two completely separate issues, many previously complicated problems became surprisingly clear. My work with clients became more focused in the specific aspects of their needs. I found that when I viewed the two as separate, yet interrelated, people began to understand what I was saying.

The concepts of self-esteem and self-love are integrated, but they are not one and the same. Self-esteem is extremely important and can lead to the deeper expression of self-love. Let's say self-esteem is the flower and loving oneself is the deep, rich color and the subtle fragrance. Can we have one without the other? Do you have to be able to touch the flower to experience its beauty? If you see the flower, but cannot smell its fragrance, does that mean it is not there? Can it possibly mean that more development in your senses will help you distinguish its lovely perfume?

Learning to love ourselves, to smell the delicate fragrance of this unique perfume, should be an important part of any therapeutic process. It has traditionally been called "self-esteem work." Actually, beginning to focus self-love as an important therapeutic outcome makes it happen with purpose rather than as a fortunate by-product of other important work.

When I began to see the separateness of self-esteem and self-love, cases that previously seemed so muddy became clear. In working with a wide variety of therapeutic issues, I found that separating these two concepts helped tremendously. In working with eating disorders, my focus, over the years, moved into the complicated, painful areas of compulsive eating and obesity.

There is a common phenomenon in the area of eating disorder work related to obesity that fits the concept of looking at self-esteem and self-love as separate issues. Many people struggling with obesity are extremely intelligent, capable individuals with basically good self-esteem. Along with these strong characteristics often come a deep self-loathing and hatred. It is almost like being split into two people, without the disassociative response of Multiple Personality Disorder.

The people who struggle with the intense pain of obesity usually enter therapy very confused about themselves. The initial request for therapy is usually motivated by the hope, once again, that this path will be the one to permanent weight loss. This, the pursuit of the "real me" who is slim and able to reflect the "me I think is hiding inside" is what they are seeking without always being able to say the words aloud. They have spent years, sometimes a lifetime, trying to sort themselves out. They are asking, "What part of me is me? Am I my fat, my feelings, my abilities, or all of these? If I am very capable and talented, but I look 'like this' (stated with intense self-loathing), does any of the good stuff count?"

One part of the person in this dilemma is extremely successful, well-respected, intelligent, creative, and organized at work and usually at home. The other part feels frightened, grotesquely obvious, uncomfortable, inadequate, and loathsome. The organized, intelligent side will take all the logical steps necessary to "eat healthy and take care of oneself," while it struggles with the side that rebels, sabotages, and feels deprived and angry.

The frequency of high self-esteem is seldom acknowledged in the literature and research on obesity. This may be because it is easy to assume that someone who doesn't possess self-love also has no self-confidence, and therefore, no self-esteem. Separating the two concepts helps to validate the strengths and focus the work where it is truly needed, on learning to accept and love oneself.

Many of the weight loss and fitness centers structure their advertising to appeal to the fearful, desperate side of the people who loathe their bodies, while they structure their programs with the intelligent, capable, organized side of these people in mind. The part of the person that needs the help, the part that does not have a clue how to achieve self-love, is rarely or adequately addressed. When both sides of this enigma are not addressed, the client often "fails by program standards" or cannot keep the weight off and ends up fueling those feelings of self-hatred. Something is missing. Any of us who have done the "diet, gain it, lose it again, hate myself, diet, gain lots more, hate myself even more, give up, refuse to diet, feel desperate, organize it, lose it, panic, start it all over again syndrome" knows exactly what I'm talking about.

To very capable people, it is a relief to hear that self-esteem is not always the problem. Self-esteem is affected by their issue of not yet loving themselves, but it should not necessarily be the focus of therapy. This helps them truly be able to put aside that strong portion of their personalities and be vulnerable enough to look deeply into their emotional feelings about themselves. Some people view this strong, capable part as a "mask" they wear, and their true self is that fearful person inside. There is a secret fear that if someone ever caught a glimpse of that "loathsome creature" inside, there would be immediate rejection and abandonment. These feelings can be even more magnified if that person has already felt rejected for a more obvious condition such as obesity, a physical challenge, or some aspect of their physical appearance.

It seems odd to think that a person who has basically good self-esteem could actually feel hate or loathing in another area of personal development. It is just this perception that gives us all the feeling that we need to hide that "real" self inside for fear of being discovered. When someone says to another "you have it all together, it must be great not to ever feel bad or doubt yourself," the pressure is even greater to "keep up the mask" and shove the difficult feelings inside.

The structure of our diagnostic criteria in the field of psychology makes it difficult to honor the strong, capable part of a person while treating the vulnerable, traumatized part inside. Convention (and insurance companies) would deny a diagnosis of "a high-functioning person, with a strong, positive, well-developed self-esteem who has a problem with self-loathing, fear of abandonment, and rejection in a limited part of their personal makeup." To conform to our current standard of mental health care, we are supposed to treat and focus on the weakness and categorize it into an acceptable diagnosis such as depression, anxiety, or some other mental illness or disorder.

The people who have good self-esteem are actually well on their way to working through their issues and moving into a place of truly loving themselves. Since they have already accomplished the difficult aspect of basically believing in who they are and their capabilities, they can begin to move into working on whatever is blocking them from loving themselves. If we simply remove the imagined wall that separates this strong outer personality (the mask) from the part of ourselves that we tend to view as "real" (the vulnerable one inside), then we begin to see that we are not really separate but one within ourselves. Then we don't have to wait until we are "all perfect" through and through to begin to love who we are.

Recognition and understanding of self-esteem can lead to self-love. Developing and practicing the concepts and behaviors explained in this chapter can help you feel good about who you are. This can motivate your behavior to reflect that positive self-image. That is self-esteem. As we go over these important lessons about self-esteem, keep in mind the idea of loving yourself. Just think about it.

Parents often call me requesting therapy for their young children and adolescents. "She doesn't have any self-esteem" or "it is so obvious that he really doesn't like himself" are common phrases in their description of the problems for which they seek help. I usually ask "How so?" or "What is it that makes you know this?" The answers I get are usually a variety of questionable behaviors, school problems, attitudes, and depressive symptoms such as withdrawal, isolation, crying a lot, appetite disturbances, and more.

In these children, as well as the adults with whom I work, the most common factor I have found is a lack of self-confidence. Self-esteem is not a prerequisite for self-confidence, but self-confidence is a prerequisite for self-esteem. In other words, you can believe in your abilities and not feel good about yourself, but it is very difficult to feel good about yourself if you don't believe in your abilities. Thought provoking, isn't it?

The other main obstacle to people loving themselves is that they don't feel they deserve to be loved. There is a deep, core issue of feeling "unlovable." This can come from childhood issues created by a lack of love, but it can also come from a failure to forgive ourselves for past mistakes and problems. These issues can be addressed in therapy to create a freedom to experience love, maybe for the first time. Finding the core issue that is hindering self-love can be a tremendously freeing experience.

The following client was a 16-year-old girl who believed in her capabilities but did not like herself very much. She knew she was capable of doing many things extremely well but saw herself as unlovable.

Lauren, age 16, was brought in to see me by her father and her stepmother due to their concerns about her lack of self-esteem. Lauren's mother had died in a car accident when she was a baby, and her stepmother was the only mother she had ever known. It was confusing to her parents and the school counselor that she did not seem to like herself because she was attractive, athletic, intelligent, and popular. Lauren seemed to succeed at everything she did. In spite of her many attributes, Lauren consistently put herself down and felt awful about herself.

When I began seeing Lauren, she was able to tell me all the things she could do. She believed in her abilities in many different areas and had confidence about dealing with her world. This true, outward confidence masked an underlying feeling that she was unlovable. She knew that her family loved her, as she did them, and felt that her good friends loved her as well, although she couldn't understand why they did. Lauren told me that she liked who she was on the outside but did not feel like a very good person on the inside. She had no conscious reasons that she could think of that would justify her negative inner feelings.

Lauren willingly went along with my suggestion that we do some hypnosis to see if we could uncover some subconscious process that was influencing her opinion of herself. For three sessions we found nothing remarkable, except an improvement in Lauren's awareness of her problem and a deepening conviction to discover why she felt that way.

During our fourth hypnosis session, Lauren relaxed easily into our routine and found herself in a quiet, peaceful place. I encouraged her to look around and see what was presented to her. From her trance state, she told me that she heard a baby crying. I suggested she follow the cries.

As Lauren followed the cries of the baby, she said that the sky began to darken, and she was feeling frightened. I encouraged her to stay with it. She came upon an hysterically crying baby strapped in a car seat. Lauren began to cry softly as she stared at the child. "I don't want to touch her. I'll scare her more," Lauren sobbed.

"What does she need?" I coached.

"I don't know. I don't know. She's so scared," Lauren said softly as she continued to cry.

"What does a scared, crying baby need?" I asked again.

"Someone to pick her up and hold her. Someone just to love her and let her know she's okay." Lauren followed my directions to do what she had suggested. In the big, brown recliner in my office, Lauren sobbed clutching a pillow to her chest. I waited.

After some time, the crying slowly stopped and Lauren sat calmly in the chair with her eyes softly focused on the table in front of her. She had brought herself out of the trance. Lauren looked at me and said softly, "That was me, wasn't it?"

"Tell me about your experience," I encouraged.

"I think that was me when I was little, after my mom was killed in the car accident. Maybe I missed her, or maybe I didn't understand why she was gone. I don't know. I only know that the little baby in the car seat was terribly afraid. When I unstrapped her and picked her up, I started crying as I held her. By the time I came out of it, here in your office, I couldn't tell who was the baby and who was me. I think it was me, now, holding that little baby that was me, then. I feel so different, like someone has lifted a big weight off of me."

The following week, Lauren came into her session with her father in tow. "I brought my dad in to tell you what he told me after I explained last week's hyp-

nosis session to him," Lauren said excitedly.

Lauren's father proceeded to explain to me that he felt compelled to tell Lauren the rest of the story about her mother's death, after Lauren shared her hypnosis experience about the baby in the car seat. It turned out that Lauren had been in the car with her mother at the time of the accident. Somehow, Lauren's car seat had been ejected from the car during the accident, and she was found several yards away, next to the road, crying. It was as though someone had gently set her down next to the road. Lauren was not physically injured. It had been so traumatic for her father to lose his wife and to come so close to losing his child, that he never talked about it to Lauren. She was only told that her mother died in a car accident when she was a baby. Her father, and Lauren, reported that she seemed so much "lighter" since her discoveries last week.

Lauren's awareness and healing of that frightened little baby within her was a turning point in her therapy. After several more sessions she felt that she could allow the self-love to begin to grow and truly let the love in from the people around her. Her self-esteem improved dramatically.

Lauren's story is not as uncommon as it may seem. Of course, many of us are not as fortunate to find a specific event that has such a dramatic impact on the ability to feel self-love. It is often much more subtle and complicated, like the pieces of a puzzle that eventually fit together to form a picture that is you. A real blessing is that every single piece of the puzzle is not always necessary to see the overall picture.

Self-esteem is an aspect of personal growth that continues for the rest of our lives. This is actually good news to many people who have feared that if they didn't develop good self-esteem in childhood, they were out of luck. Knowing the characteristics involved in developing your self-esteem can help clarify where you are now and where you are headed. A simplistic hierarchy of self-esteem development can be stated as follows:

BEGINNING LEVEL of SELF-ESTEEM DEVELOPMENT

Feelings of inadequacy and unimportance.
Low functioning within personal environment.
No eye contact.

INTERMEDIATE LEVEL of SELF-ESTEEM DEVELOPMENT

Hesitant feelings of success.
Beginning feelings of self-respect.
Functions well within personal environment.
Eye contact with trusted people.

ADVANCED LEVEL of SELF-ESTEEM

Feelings of accomplishment and success.
Self-respect.
Respected by others.
High functioning within personal environment.
Good eye contact with people in general.

How do we know which level we fall into? The simplest way to determine whether your self-esteem is positively or negatively developed is to listen to the person who knows you the best -- yourself. Tune into that little voice in the back of your head and see what you have to say. Go ahead, you'll recognize some key words and phrases if you really listen.

This inner voice is called our "self-talk." It's not something others can hear, unless we slip and say it out loud, or mumble it under our breath, but we hear it loud and clear. If others did hear it, and thought you were talking to them, they would most likely be extremely insulted. The things we say to ourselves are not usually very nice.

Remember how the cartoons would depict a character struggling with some dilemma? The little angel would stand on one shoulder and the little devil on the other. Each would try to plead, convince, coerce, and harass the character into taking some action. We would laugh and say, "I do that to myself," and promptly put the awareness out of our minds. This was an animation of "self-talk." It was easy to understand what we were seeing because everyone really does that. No one stopped to consider if this was a good thing to do; it was simply a part of our being. We did not realize that talking to ourselves in this way could be hurting our developing self-esteem.

The problem is this -- we are so accustomed to our own self-talk that we think it, hear it, and promptly tune it out of our consciousness. Our subconscious is always listening and responds accordingly, directing us to the thing we've focused on the most. If you tell someone "do not think about pink elephants" over and over again, it will be hard for them not to think about pink elephants. You are continually focusing attention on them. It works the same way with our self-talk.

Imagine telling your 3-year-old every morning, "Now Sweetie, I don't want you to stick any bobby pins in that nasty little electric outlet today. It will hurt if you do." Every time your 3-year-old sees an electric outlet, what thoughts do you think will be going through his head? We tend to move in the direction on which we focus our attention.

The first time I became aware of my negative self-talk, I was "knee-deep" in a destructive eating disorder. I would look in the mirror and think some very nasty, harsh things about my physical appearance. At the same time, I felt good about my 4.0 grade point average, putting myself through college, my musical abilities, my job, my friends, my family, and much more. This high-functioning, confident, attractive young woman -- "me" -- was ruthlessly ripping herself apart every time she looked into the mirror. At the time it felt like the right thing was to "do something" to fix what I perceived was wrong. At 5'3", 112 pounds, I was sure that I was fat. What I did not understand at the time was that I was pulling myself into a "negatively spiraling cycle" that would take years to overcome.

I focused with such intensity on what I feared the most that I created and manipulated it into my very being. I would stand in front of the mirror and do what many years later, in my work with others, I appropriately named *"the F & U's."* This stands for the *"FAT and UGLIES."* Great term, isn't it? It has that appropriate ring of a swear word and so accurately depicts what exactly is being said within the head, which is the self-talk of someone who struggles with weight issues.

I did the "F & U's" with such vigor and venom that it

became a way of life for a long time. I couldn't look in a mirror, or my reflection in a window, for even an instant, without immediately saying something really negative to myself. Thinking back on those years now makes me feel sad, in the way one feels when seeing a bully pick on an innocent little kid. I was cruel to myself for many years before noticing what I was doing.

Tuning into your own self-talk is relatively easy. Go through your daily routines and just listen. What kind of things do you say to yourself when you:

- Look in the mirror?
- Make a mistake?
- Get a compliment?
- Have to make a speech or head a meeting?
- Turn in a report?
- Balance your checkbook?
- Confront someone who has hurt you?
- Discipline your children?
- Hang up the phone from talking to your parents?

There are thousands of things we do everyday that give us the opportunity to either tear ourselves down or build ourselves up. These situations are the ones that give us the opportunity to listen to ourselves -- to tune into our self-talk -- to see what words we use to judge ourselves. Some typical, negative phrases people working on their self-talk share with me are: "I'll never make it"; "I am so stupid"; "no one will want me"; and "I am worthless to everyone." This is just a small sampling and actually very mild compared to all the things people have confessed that they say to themselves.

If you list the key phrases of the self-talk you hear from yourself, you'll quickly learn a lot about your self-esteem. The areas where you have self-confidence will usually have at least some positive remarks. Your weak areas will most likely be mean and nasty. Most things we say to ourselves when we are not meeting our own expectations are things people generally would not say to any other person in their adult world.

Interestingly enough though, some people say the same, horrible, negative things that they say to themselves to their children. Can it be that they heard these comments from their own parents and are now keeping them alive within themselves and passing them on to the next generation? "You're never going to amount to anything if you don't get off your fat, lazy butt and do something constructive." "How do you ever expect to get anywhere in life with grades like these?" These types of demeaning comments can become the negative self-talk in adulthood that sounds like "I've never amounted to anything" and "I'm basically a lazy person" and even the good old standby, "I hate my fat butt."

I have often asked clients, after we've reviewed their list of negative self-talk comments, if they would want to say these things to their children. They always say, "No!" When I ask them why, they usually say they don't want to ruin their self-esteem.

Our self-talk directly influences our self-esteem. If you've just spent five or ten minutes, or five or ten years, or a lifetime, ripping yourself apart, how do you feel about yourself? Not too good, do you? When you feel like you've just been beaten emotionally, your confidence in yourself and your abilities plummets. Imagine this:

"Okay, honey, it's time to leave for school. This is your first day of kindergarten, aren't you excited? Now listen and remember that you are really dumb and pretty ugly, too. No one is going to like you because you dress weird and you have a big nose and your ears stick out. Your hair didn't go quite right, so remember to be really self-conscious of it all day. If the teacher calls on you, everyone will probably find out that you're really stupid, so it would be better if you didn't open your mouth. Besides, your teeth are ugly, too. Okay, sweetie, have a good day at school and remember, mommy loves you."

Just how confident would this kid feel after a brutal, verbal beating like that one? Imagine how you feel after you've done your own version of negative self-talk?

"This dress looks horrible on me. When I walk out of my office, I just know everyone will be staring at my fat butt. I'll have to make sure no one is behind me if I walk down the hallway. Look at my hair!! I hate my hair!! It never does what I want it to do. What's wrong with me? Why can't I make it look as good as the beautician does? I'm just not very coordinated. Maybe its my ears that make my hair go funny right there? I hate my ears!! Oh, well, I guess I'm not only butt-ugly, but I'm getting old, too. (Heavy sigh.) I better be careful not to smile when I head that meeting today or everyone will notice that I should have had braces. I hope they don't notice how fat I look in this stupid dress. Maybe I should change."

Negative self-talk lowers self-esteem in the same way that verbally abusing people hurts their self-esteem. Most people would not even begin to talk to others as negatively as they talk to themselves. Those people who regularly talk to others negatively have significant problems and must have extremely negative self-talk of their own.

If our self-talk directly influences our self-esteem, then what happens to us when our self-esteem is affected? Our self-esteem is what directs our actual behavior in the world. If our self-esteem is low, then our behavior will tend to be low functioning as well. When our behavior stinks, we tend to say some harsh things to ourselves, and then the cycle starts all over. This becomes that negatively, spiraling cycle I was referring to earlier. Let's take an example:

Jane decided that she had to go on a very strict diet. The level of the "F & U's" she had been doing when looking in the mirror had reached that well-known panic level and desperation that "diet time" was at hand once again. Just this morning she took one look at her stomach and told herself that some-one could easily mistake her for a woman that was five months pregnant. She also believed that her back-side was disgusting and her double chin made her look 10 years older.

"That's it. I am disgusting. I can't live in this body one more day," Jane declared aloud. "I'm starting my diet right now so don't plan on having anything good in this house for awhile." She actually felt good. The decision to take charge felt powerful.

As Jane entered the third day of her regimen, the sugar withdrawals and self-doubts hit about the same

time. Her ability to force her behavior into a precon-
ceived mold became more and more difficult. With
each "lapse" in control, her self-talk became even
more negative. "I am so bad. I can't even do this
one simple thing. What is wrong with me? I am so
weak. I have absolutely no self-control. This is never
going to work. Why even try? I'm going to look like a
fat pig forever, so I might as well just give it up."

It didn't take long for Jane's "dieting behavior" to
fall apart because her beliefs in herself were that she
wasn't capable of it and it would never work. Jane
ended her attempt at forcing her behavior into some
role with her self-esteem even lower and her self-talk
more negative. She said to herself, "See, I knew it
wouldn't work." The downward, spiraling cycle continued.

Negative self-talk leads to a lowering of self-esteem
which leads to negative behaviors, which then leads to more
negative self-talk. This negative cycle becomes the downward spiral of self-destruction that many have come to accept as their life. It isn't as hard as one may think to turn
this cycle into a positive spiral which leads to increased self-
esteem and improved, healthier behaviors. The key is in
your self-talk, not in trying to force yourself into behaving in
some certain manner.

Step one to improving your self-talk is "awareness."
Once you become aware of the things you say to yourself,
you can begin to stop saying the negative ones. If you think
of negative self-talk as hitting yourself over the head with a
hammer, it stands to reason that once you discover that this

hammer causes much of your pain and suffering, you would want to put it down and stop hitting yourself. If words were as tangible as a hammer in your hand, it would probably be that easy. Since words are more illusive, you will have to be diligent in continuing to notice when you have that hammer in your hand -- I mean those thoughts in your head. When you find yourself swinging away, simply say, "I have that hammer in my hand again, and I have chosen not to do that to myself anymore." You may even want to apologize to yourself, which would be a little like my talking to myself on my voice mail. What could it hurt?

Controlling the "self-abuse hammer" significantly reduces the negative self-talk. This helps you to hear it if you slip up and hit yourself again. Now you can begin to introduce the positive, uplifting self-talk that will enhance your self-esteem. If you have any doubts about what positive self-talk should sound like, listen to yourself talk to a beloved child or your best friend. Be loving, kind, and sincere. Do not lie to yourself or to your best friend. If there is something difficult or critical to be said, choose your words carefully, with love, and say it without being vindictive, mean, or sarcastic.

What a difference in the internal feelings when you hear something kind and positive. "It's okay. I'm doing the best that I can and that's what matters. I could try a little harder in this area, and that may improve things even more. I'll just take it a little at a time. I know I can do it." When your self-talk is on the right track, your self-esteem will become healthier. Positive self-talk and good self-esteem lead to positive, healthy behaviors, which give you more opportunities to say nice things to yourself. Now we have the upward, positively spiraling cycle of a growing and developing self-esteem.

The most important thing to keep in mind about self-esteem is that it is relative to who you are as a person, not how you feel you are compared to everyone else in the world. Self-esteem is not reserved only for those who are gifted in some area, talented, or physically attractive. It does not depend on your intelligence, skills, attributes, or capabilities. **SELF-ESTEEM DEPENDS ON YOUR PERCEPTIONS AND BELIEFS IN YOURSELF.** Most of us know that this is true, for other people, but do not allow it to be a personal truth.

We have all known people who do not seem to have anything remarkable or special about them, yet, they appear to have good self-esteem. They look people in the eye when they talk and appear at ease in their world. Their self-confidence is evident in their positive beliefs about their own attributes and abilities. You may envy their self-assuredness and peacefulness and wonder what it is that makes them feel so good about themselves. These are the people who appear to become more and more attractive as you get to know them. Their qualities shine through and their negative characteristics seem to diminish. Their self-esteem can make them extremely interesting and attractive to other people. You would probably assume that they love themselves. It is astonishing to discover that many people with great self-esteem do not truly love themselves.

We can have all the self-esteem in the world, but if we are unable to let these good thoughts of ourselves into our hearts and embrace them as valuable and true, our self-esteem does nothing to help us develop self-love. The people who have good self-esteem, but little self-love, will typically tell you their attributes with a "but" attached to the end of their statement. "I'm extremely efficient, hard-working, and loyal at work, but..." or "I'm a good wife and mother and well respected at my job, but..." or "I'm good at the things I do in my life, but..." The negating of themselves that they do aloud is exactly what occurs inside their heads with their self-talk. "I may be good at things on the outside, but I'm really not very lovable on the inside" is what they are usually trying to say.

After we have worked on our skills, attributes, and abilities to help us gain self-esteem, or after we've realized we always have had good self-esteem, how do we go about learning this elusive concept called "self-love?" There isn't any special technique or behavior to establish. It is actually not a skill at all but a simple shift in perception that makes loving ourselves possible.

PERFECT LOVE

In Chapter One we looked at the concepts of Love and Fear. Existing in a place of Fear regarding ourselves would preclude loving ourselves. If we embrace the idea that the world we know was created in "Perfect Love" and anything that is not of "Perfect Love" is not of that original creation, and therefore of Fear, then we are off to a good start with the concept of learning to love ourselves.

Some people will have trouble accepting the idea of a world created in "Perfect Love." You can put this philosophy into any religious or spiritual context you desire. If you need to, you can even take the concept outside any spiritual context and look at it as a philosophical viewpoint. It really doesn't matter how, why, or from what viewpoint you explore the idea of a world of perfect love; simply allow yourself to drop your shields and take a look. Consider this concept -- **What if the world were created in "Perfect Love?"**

If "Fear" is what we call anything that is not part of the "Perfect Love," it becomes easier to see that if we don't feel love for ourselves then we must be in a place of "Fear." Look at "Fear" as something that was created by us, as human beings, to try to justify, understand, explain, and control the challenges and difficulties in life. That makes it easier to understand how we can so easily get stuck in that place and lose sight of the fact that we, along with everything else, were created in "Perfect Love." Think of that popular saying "I must be okay because God doesn't make any mistakes." "Perfect Love" is the same concept simply expressed with different words.

"Do you love yourself?" I asked the 48-year-old man sitting in front of me in my office.

He looked at me with a startled expression and replied, "I have a lot of things I like about myself. I'm intelligent, I'm a good father and husband, plus I think I have some positive characteristics like honesty and loyalty. I've done really well in my business and I'm proud of that." His expression seemed to say that he was certain he had answered my question.

"Yes, you have excellent self-esteem," I replied, "but, do you love yourself?"

"Maybe I don't know what you mean. Are you asking me if I like myself?"

"I'm asking you if you love yourself. What does loving someone mean to you?"

He thought for a few moments and said, "I love

my wife and children. It's easy for me to say that and know what I mean. It's hard to put into words exactly how I know this, but I do know that I love them."

"Do you think about yourself in the same way?" I asked.

"Heavens no," he replied without hesitation, "I know too much about myself." He laughed lightly and then became serious again. "I've made mistakes in my life and done some things that I'm not too proud of, so it would be hard to really feel totally loving of myself."

"Have others you loved ever made mistakes?"

"Of course," he sighed, obviously aware of where I was going with this, "and no, I haven't stop loving them when they made a mistake."

Knowing that this man was extremely spiritual with a deep faith in God, I asked him if he thought God had forgiven him for his mistakes and wrong-doings.

"I know He has forgiven me. I have no doubt about it," he stated with confidence.

"Does God love you?"

"Of course, I truly believe God loves all of us," he said quietly. "I see what I've been doing. All of a sudden it is so obvious. I believe God forgives me and loves me, but I haven't allowed myself to do the same thing."

"So you know better than God?" I replied with a smile. "Who died and left you the job," we both said simultaneously and laughed.

If we can grasp the concept that our world was created in "Perfect Love," then anything that is not of "Love" must be of "Fear." If you don't truly love yourself, then the next logical question would be, "What are you afraid of?"

I sense fear from people all the time. They are afraid that if they were ever to lighten up on themselves, they would lose any desire or motivation to change. I see this attitude associated with all types of problems. A woman struggling with the negative self-talk regarding a weight problem is afraid to stop telling herself that she's "fat and ugly." She fears becoming comfortable and that she will stop trying to lose weight, or worse, gain more. The executive continuously tells himself that he is not as far along in his career as he "should" be and that he isn't going to amount to anything. He fears he may become satisfied with his current position and salary if he stops the self-condemnations.

One of the many blessings of the innocence of childhood is that very young children seldom have fears of not being good enough. These fears are learned behaviors that are modeled in our environment and are all around us. We learn early to run faster, earn more, weigh less, acquire more, be better, learn more, don't stop, and for heaven's sake, don't ever get comfortable with yourself. The subtle message is that if you ever get comfortable with yourself, then you are lazy or not striving to be the absolute best that you can be. "There is always room for improvement" seems to be the motto of our era. Our children learn this lesson quickly, and the pressure and stress begin to mount at earlier and earlier ages.

The discipline style 40 to 50 years ago and before that was "if the child is doing something right, be quiet, because if you say something he'll stop doing it." Most children heard only what they were doing incorrectly or what they needed to improve. When Behaviorism came into vogue, the concept of "positive reinforcement" took hold, and child rearing became more positive. Research showed that if you told someone what they were doing right, there was a greater chance of that person doing it right again. Children began to be congratulated, or reinforced, for what they did right.

I believe many people are generally aware of the concept of positive reinforcement, but since it does take some extra effort, it is not what occurs in most of our lives all the time. When my teenager cleans the bathroom, I sometimes need to remind myself several times to compliment her on the things she does well. My inclination is to walk in the room to check her work and simply say, "You missed cleaning around the faucets." Employers attend seminars to learn positive management styles. Parents attend classes to become better parents. Teachers are encouraged to build self-esteem through positive reinforcement in the classrooms.

With the increased awareness that positive feedback creates a rise in self-esteem, why are so many people still so hesitant to love themselves? It makes sense that if we relax and allow ourselves to feel loved and safe, we perform at our best with less effort. All the energy we spend beating ourselves up and putting ourselves down can be channeled into productive self-growth and change. Imagine employers, parents, and teachers not only promoting self-esteem but also encouraging people to love themselves.

Loving ourselves does not mean we give up any desires for improvement, growth, or change. It simply means that we love ourselves, meaning our true "self," as we are, without constantly being afraid that we are not going to be good enough. That's how good, loving parents raise their children. We don't hold back our love because our children have growing and changing to do and improvements to make. We don't fear letting them know we are proud of them or impressed with their accomplishments, for fear that telling them these things may make them stagnate and unwilling to change. We know that building their self-esteem will make even more of the good things available within them to fuel positive growth and change.

Wouldn't it be wonderful if we allowed self-love to happen in the same way that we so lovingly try to raise our children? What if we cherished ourselves and treated our own souls with gentleness, kindness, and sensitivity? We can talk to ourselves with positive overtones and encourage ourselves to be the best that we can be. Occasionally, when we least expect it, we can leave ourselves a message that simply says, "I love you."

Self-Esteem Cycle

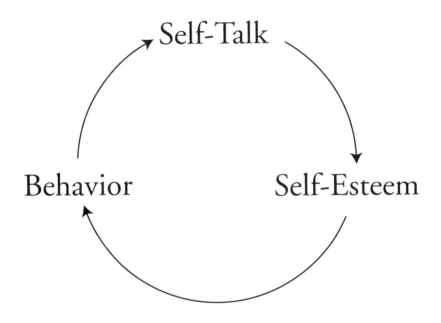

Self-Talk

Self-Esteem

Behavior

Negatively Spiraling Cycle

Positively Spiraling Cycle

SELF-TALK

↓

SELF-CONFIDENCE

↓

SELF-ESTEEM

↓

SELF-ACCEPTANCE

↓

SELF-LOVE

CHAPTER TEN

THE ROAD TO LOVE

*"Be watchful,
stand firm in your faith,
be courageous, be strong.
Let all that you do
be done in love."
-- I Corinthians 16:13-14*

The "Road to Love" is an incredible discovery that is waiting for each of us. The lessons you have learned in this book will help prepare you to become aware of this path, find it for yourself, and hone the skills that will help you know when you are there and when you stray. The road to "Nowhere" can be a nasty place, but it is never too late to find your way to the "Road to Love." It is on this wondrous, loving path that you will feel calmer inside and more positive about life. When we each choose to open our eyes to "Love," we answer our unspoken question -- "How can I feel better about my life?" The answer to our question is "Love." The answer to our pain, heartache, trauma, losses, and fear is "Love." The answer is always "Love."

In Chapter One we discussed the definition of "Love" and found that it was a seemingly complex topic that was difficult to define. In learning about some of the many areas of self-growth, it becomes apparent that each one leads to "Love" and creates a much broader meaning than seemed possible before these lessons were learned.

It is very important to recognize that "Love" is not a destination that anyone obtains, it is a path to follow -- a journey -- to explore and experience. On this wondrous road there can be difficult challenges that seem to block our way and feel hazardous to our safety. These are the opportunities placed before us that allow the new skills and insights to be used to meet these invitations to self-growth.

Freedom from "Fear" can be obtained by the simple alteration of seeing the obstacles that are placed before us on our "Road to Love" as gifts of opportunity, instead of bad luck or punishments. Over and over again we are given the opportunity to grow and learn the lessons we chose to discover when our souls entered our physical bodies. If we miss a chance to learn, the lesson seems to present itself again, often bigger, louder, and more noticeable than the first time. Ask yourself, "Do I want to wait until this lesson comes around again to grasp the opportunity it is offering to me?"

The idea of our lessons being offered over and over again, until we finally notice and learn from them, is a little scary and comforting at the same time. If we fail to notice an opportunity, we can feel confident that it will come around again in possibly another form. It's a nifty little concept but does not always feel so good when something comes around to "bite you in the butt" for the second, third, fourth, fifth (need I go on?) time.

Consider this possibility...

The 7-year-old boy watched the money fall from the man's pocket as he sat down on the bench. The boy waited patiently until the man left and then put the bills in his own pocket...

The 12-year-old boy noticed that the cashier gave him change for a 20-dollar bill instead of a 10 -- he bit his tongue and hurried out of the store...

The teenage boy talked furiously to justify why his time card did not fit his hours worked at his new job. He felt clever at fooling the manager with his quick explanations...

The 20-year-old college student is angry that his professor gave him a failing grade on his term paper because the professor recognized it as one that was written several years earlier by an honor student...

The 30-year-old stresses during the tax audit of his liberally fantasized and undocumented returns...

The 40-year-old is angry at the breakup of his third marriage and thinks women should know that monogamy is impossible...

The 70-year-old lies in his pauper's bed, dying alone, thinking "I had a hard life and it wasn't fair."

"Love" means so many things regarding how we feel, how we behave, and how we believe. Another way to view this paradigm is with the well-known concept of "Mind, Body, and Spirit."

Spirit

- Life is a journey...
- A world created in perfect love...
- The gift of opportunity in the form of a challenge...

Love

Mind

- Honor
- Integrity
- Trust
- Self-Esteem
- Self-Love
- Intimacy

Body

- Relaxation
- Exercise
- Eating Healthy
- Illness as an opportunity
- Intimacy

If you look at the structure of the "Mind, Body, Spirit" diagram, you'll notice that it is a triangle. Each side of this concept rests upon the other. If one side were missing, the whole thing would collapse. It's the same with our self-growth. We must develop in all three of these areas -- mind, body and spirit -- in order to be well balanced. This balancing of our lives is one of the paths that lead to our "Road to Love."

If we focus only on our mind and develop that aspect of who we are, we quickly find areas of weakness in our body and lack of spiritual development or awareness. It is equally so if we only focus on the body or outward appearances. We will lack in intellectual/emotional and spiritual growth. The same is true for those who are totally focused on spiritual issues. Their life will lack the wholeness that is required to be a well-balanced individual.

Each side of the "Mind, Body, Spirit" triangle relies on the strength of the other to hold the structure in balance. If energy is put into all three areas, allowing us to nurture each aspect of our development, we will grow in a healthy, well-balanced way.

Most parents encourage this balanced type of growth in their children. We want them to eat healthy and get plenty of exercise playing outside in the fresh air and sunshine. We want them to be careful so as not to be injured or sick. Education, skills, talents, and new insights are encouraged as we try to teach them how to live and succeed in the world. Spiritual beliefs are taught. Sometimes these beliefs are given in the form of formal religious training. Sometimes they are presented in a more subtle, quiet manner of talking to the children about how you believe the world operates. Would you ever consider leaving out any one of these important areas of growth? You instinctively know that a child would not be able to survive very successfully in the world without some basic training in each of these areas.

As it is with the children, so it is with the adults. The lessons do not stop when we leave our parents' care and go out into the world on our own. We are constantly being given the lessons and opportunities for growth in each of the areas of mind, body, and spirit. We simply need to notice them in order to avail ourselves of the complete experience.

In order to experience lasting change within ourselves and our lives, we must accomplish the spiritual task of allowing ourselves to change our thoughts, beliefs, and attitudes. This change is the purpose of the gifts of lessons and opportunities that will guide us in our growth. This change brings us to the "Road to Love."

Everyone, at times, needs the guidance and assistance of someone else to help in this path of change and self-growth. These teachers come to us in many forms. Often they are people in our lives, but they can be many, many other things. Animals, books, movies, places, music, poetry, and art are just a few of the possible teachers we seek in our lives. All of these teachers are there to help us find our spiritual connection.

I often use a simple visual tool with the people I see who are working on their spiritual development. The image shows each of us being spiritually connected with God. People call God by many names. You can call this energy the Holy Spirit, Jesus, God, your Higher Power, Buddha, Allah, "All That Is," or numerous other titles. The name you call this connection is unimportant. What matters is that you allow the connection to be a part of your life.

Blocking yourself off from your spiritual connection leaves you isolated and stagnating in your energy. The renewal of energy that occurs when we are on the "Road to Love" is something that you miss terribly if you lose it. Once you know what it feels like to let this incredible "Perfect Love" into your heart, you do not want to risk losing it by taking a side road to "Nowhere." The fantastic thing is that it is there for each of us if we only get out of the way and let it in.

Finding a path to Love does not have to fit into any specific religious organization. It is available to anyone and everyone without offending any spiritual orientation. On your path you may embrace any organized religious beliefs or none if you prefer. That is a choice that is extremely personal and totally up to you.

The "Road to Love " is not something that we can simply achieve in a series of lessons or behavioral steps, although they are very important in helping us get there. The "Road to Love" exists and waits for us to see its existence. When we are ready to "allow" it to be true for us, it will be so by a simple shift in attitude -- a quantum leap of faith. Then our skills, tools, and lessons learned will be available to us to help us on this path.

Seeing every situation from a place of "Love" and being "perfect" on this journey are not what this is all about. We all make mistakes, and sometimes we even leave the main road and take that destructive side road to "Nowhere." The key is to learn from these challenging and sometimes painful side roads. We must use the tools to return, once again, to the "Road to Love."

Very few ever achieve a total state of enlightenment

whereby they never again veer from this chosen path. Most of us are simply trying to survive doing this "human thing" and can only strive to do the best we possibly can with what we have learned so far.

When I'm feeling a little bit "full of myself," I like to take a minute to look at the "drop in the bucket." This is a mental picture of a bucket of water. I am but one molecule in one drop of water in this bucket. My circle of influence in the environment consists of the other molecules in this single drop. Backing up the view from the molecule, to the single drop, to the entire contents of the bucket, it becomes apparent how each of us is a small, yet integral part of the whole. Now back up even further, like a rocket soaring into space. The bucket is now a minuscule thing on the Earth. Zooming into space, the entire picture becomes a tiny part of the whole universe. At the same time it becomes clear that each of us is a part of the whole -- of all that is.

Our tiny part matters. Creating "Love" within our single molecule of existence affects the entire drop. One drop of "Love" in this bucket, joined by other drops, begins to affect the entire bucket. Creating a world -- a universe -- of "Love" begins with the tiniest part -- YOU!!

EPILOGUE

EPILOGUE

If the <u>Therapy In A Nutshell</u> journey has captured your attention, you will have learned — or started to learn — the skills to help live life from a place of Love. It is my hope that you will read this book again at different periods during your life and understand it from a deeper level each time.

A summary of the <u>10 Simple Lessons That Will Change Your Life</u> may be valuable as a checklist or reminder during difficult challenges.

LESSON 1: Learn to recognize Fear for what it really is — mistrust. Let go of the "Illusions of Safety" to move into a place of Love.

LESSON 2: The five "Trusting Levels" help create healthy personal interactions with reasonable and appropriate expectations and behaviors.

LESSON 3: The patterns of conscious and unconscious thoughts and behaviors affect our emotional growth and development.

LESSON 4: Healthy, mindful risk taking can enliven our lives and give us opportunities to love.

LESSON 5: Simplifying life — getting rid of the "ten in three" — reduces stress and makes room to live life from a place of Love.

LESSON 6: We must understand the past and turn toward the future as we enjoy the journey of life in the here and now.

LESSON 7: Living a personal life of honor and integrity from a place of Love is one of our primary challenges.

LESSON 8: Honoring your relationships with personal skills of integrity, independence and healthy interdependence is important. As we learn to love others, we fulfill one of the primary purposes of our Earthly existence.

LESSON 9: Self-esteem is important but not enough. The true goal is to love yourself unconditionally.

LESSON 10: All the lessons lead to one place — a place of Love. Learning to see this road and walk its path is that primary purpose in our life. This is the "Road to Love." Let all that we do be done in Love.

This is the gift. It was given to me to give to you. In the giving of it I have received a bounty of blessings in my heart. Thank you for sharing this journey with me.

With Love,

Patty Bay

THE ROAD TO LOVE

The road to love
Can be seen,
As a path to follow
From which we glean
Many wondrous, valuable tools
To live our lives by loving rules.

The blocks, pitfalls
And hazards found,
Are simply challenges that abound
To give our lives that gentle lift,
To see the love that is our gift.

The path to nowhere,
So barren and burned
Leads us astray
From all we've learned.

This tempting avenue
Filled with deceit
Seems so pleasant at our feet.
But soon the heartache, pain and strife
Begin to fill our daily life.

To this road of love
We can return
To the many joys there are to learn
To feel the honor of all that's right
Our souls' desire to live in light.

—Patricia L. Bay